"The U.S. Army has made it a top pri͏͏ / as competent soldiers, but also as sk͏͏ our country around the world. We use C͏͏ ͏ad-ership course. It is a great tool in bu͏͏ ls in the 21st century."

—Col. Joseph LeBoeuf,
Head, Leadership Program,
U.S. Military Academy at West Point

"Churchill used to say: 'the higher the ape climbs, the more you see of his behind.' The more today's managers work globally, the more they expose themselves to risks and hazards. This book offers essential principles and tips for senior managers who must circumnavigate the treacherous cliffs of other cultures. The graphic examples, impactful statistics and entertaining style make it an easy read. I wish I had had access to Zweifel's tools 35 years ago when I was starting out."

—**Werner Brandmayr,**
President and Managing Director,
Conoco Continental Holding GmbH

"A great read—and you end up feeling smarter as a result of it. Part of the charm of being American is being overbearing and bullish, but sometimes we don't realize the effect our behavior has on other cultures. Absolutely required reading for leaders who manage across cultures."

—**Ali Velshi, Anchor, CNNfn**

"I have been in the business of cross-border M&As for a long time. This would be great reading for our clients. For somebody who didn't grow up with this at the dining table, it's an excellent way of getting up to speed quickly. It picks out the parts of the cross-cultural puzzle and makes them understandable and usable. The section on preventing things from going wrong is an excellent analysis of elements that go into the cross-cultural melting pot. If you follow these prescriptions, you have an instant leg up on the competition. This is a great book."

—**John Adams, President, Adams & Royer, Inc.**

"Fascinating, informative, educational and thoroughly entertaining. I have worked for five decades in the international finance community—Europe, North and Latin America, and Asia. Given my experience in international dealings with people of different cultural backgrounds, I appreciate the colorful stories. Your advice, admonitions and secrets are priceless."
—Richard Murray, Vice Chairman, LaProv Corporation

"*Culture Clash* does an excellent job of delivering examples from Zweifel's practical experience and his scholarly wisdom on international management. It presents a series of thought-provoking exercises while allowing the reader to learn from the mistakes of others. You come away from the book with a rare combination of outcomes: a new perspective on American culture, a strong motivation to lead your team in any culture, and some real tools for removing your own cultural blinders."
—Dr. William J. Ball,
Director, Leadership in Public Affairs Program,
The College of New Jersey

"*Culture Clash* is worth real money for global companies. The productivity of large corporations is directly linked to culture—the more senior you are, the more you have got to pay attention to cross-cultural roadblocks. If you want to build or manage a global high-performance team, read this book and give it to everyone around you."   **—Steve Baird,**
Managing Director, Human Resources, UBS Warburg

"*Culture Clash* is the perfect book for policymakers who have to integrate different cultures to fulfill their mandates. I recommend this book and its delightful stories and useful exercises to everyone in government, which is after all about harmonizing conflict and building consensus. This book really deserves support and success."   **—Liszt Vieira,**
President of the Botanic Garden of Rio de Janeiro, Brazil,
Former Minister of Environment in the State of Rio de Janeiro

"As Japan's former chief diplomat, I have seen time and time again how small cross-cultural misunderstandings can spin out of control. We live in dangerous and turbulent times in international affairs, and we must do everything in our power to bridge cultural differences. Thomas Zweifel's book helps us do exactly that. It is an important and timely book, and it should be read by all those who are working not only to prevent culture clash, but for our common future as humanity."
— **Hon. Koji Kakizawa, Member, House of Representatives, Japan;**
former Foreign Minister, Japan;
former Member, Global Board of Directors, The Hunger Project

"*Culture Clash: Managing the Global High-Performance Team* is a fascinating and clearly written book that will greatly empower the managers of any global corporation or team. Thomas Zweifel's many years of experience working effectively in cultures all over the world has given him an uncanny and insightful access to the real and profound keys to success working cross-culturally, where a minefield of mistakes are often waiting to happen. His book is clear, concise and gets right down to the best nuggets available on this topic and he shares his insight with both wit and wisdom.

"A brilliant piece of work and highly relevant to today's global culture."
—**Lynne Twist,**
President of The Turning Tide Coalition and
author of *The Soul of Money*

"I am a big-time believer in building global competency, and have personally been through a wide range of problems you face in a cross-cultural environment. Global competency requires the careful selection and preparation of talent, but also constant learning since the environment changes all the time. *Culture Clash* is a great introduction for global executives to the many dimensions you need to play successfully in the global arena."
—**Hal Burlingame,**
former Executive Vice President, AT&T, and
currently Senior Executive Advisor, AT&T Wireless

"This is very much a message that boards of directors must understand if they are to lead their successful domestic business to become truly multinational organizations. Today, you need to build truly global governance—global teams committed to the organization's overarching objectives, but at the same time adaptive to local conditions and challenges. Tools like the spidergraph will help you do that." — **John Hall, Chief Executive Officer, Australian Institute of Company Directors**

"This book is simply amazing: very well documented, accurate and funny, easy to read and to use in my sessions. I've already recommended it to several clients who love it too. Simply outstanding!" — **Ann Crown, Cross-cultural management consultant**

CULTURE CLASH

Swiss Consulting Group Presents
The Global Leader Series™

CULTURE CLASH

Managing the Global High-Performance Team

THOMAS D. ZWEIFEL, Ph.D.

SelectBooks

Culture Clash: Managing the Global High-Performance Team
©2003 by Swiss Consulting Group, Inc.

This edition published by SelectBooks, Inc. For information address SelectBooks, Inc., New York, New York. Book trade members, please contact Select Books, Inc. for purchasing or further information.

First Edition

ISBN 1-59079-051-0

Library of Congress Cataloging-in-Publication Data

Zweifel, Thomas D., 1962–
  Culture clash : managing the global high-performance team / by Thomas D. Zweifel.-- 1st ed.
    p. cm. -- (The global leader series)
  ISBN 1-59079-051-0 (paperback)
1. International business enterprises—Management.
2. Leadership—Cross-cultural studies. 3. Intercultural communication. 4. Globalization. I. Title. II. Series.
HD62.4.Z85 2003
658'.049--dc21

2003004766

Manufactured in the United States of America

10 9 8 7 6 5 4 3 2 1

Swiss Consulting Group books are available at special discounts when purchased in bulk for premiums and sales promotions as well as for fundraising and educational use. Special editions or book excerpts can also be created to specification. For details, contact the Special Sales Director at books@swissconsulting group.com or
Swiss Consulting Group, Inc.
101 West 23 Street, #2422
New York, NY 10011 / USA

To Rani and the one million women in India
elected to panchayats (village governing councils)
in what is perhaps the greatest social experiment in history,
summoned to lead but not knowing how to lead;
who have to marshal more courage
and leadership every day
than you and I might summon in a year.

As for the best leaders, the people do not notice their existence.
The next best leaders, the people admire.
The next, the people fear, and the next the people hate.
But when the best leader's work is done,
the people say "we did it ourselves".

Lao Tzu, 6th century B.C.

Contents

Acknowledgments

I am grateful to so many people who directly or indirectly, knowingly or not, contributed to this book. Following are a few outstanding examples—

- Swiss Consulting Group's clients—including Aventis, Banana Republic, Citibank, GE Capital, General Motors, Goldman Sachs, JP Morgan, Lehman Brothers, Merrill Lynch, Nestlé, Novartis, Prudential, Siemens and UBS, as well as a host of small and medium-sized enterprises in the military, education and nongovernmental sectors—for using the knowledge and tools herein.

- Swiss Consulting Group's team and network of consultants worldwide, for constantly developing our body of knowledge and for contributing war stories to this book. In the United States, Tapas Sen, Dan Friel, Arthur Gutch, Richard Murray, Agnès Pégorier, Andrew Small, Peg Thatcher, Nick Wolfson, and Yoram Wurmser. In Belgium, Sonia De Vos. In Brazil, Johannes van de Ven. In Canada, Jillian Cohen. In France, Poriya Vaudecrane. In Germany, Aurora Matticoli and Nirit Sommerfeld. In Switzerland, Tony Bächle. In Turkey, Sinan Arslaner. In Australia, Oskar Kamber. In Kenya, Uma Kakde. In the United Kingdom, Mick Crews. I love our work together.

- Robert Hargrove and my colleagues at Masterful Coaching for the opportunity to contribute to their clients.

- Joan Holmes and the global board and staff of The Hunger Project, for giving me access to a worldwide mission two decades ago.

- Deborah Gouge, for editing early drafts. Dave Ellis, for giving me advice on the business of writing and publishing. Anne Nelson, my first journalism teacher, for encouraging me to publish my writing. Vily Bergen, for seeing me as a

fellow writer from the beginning. Julie Schwartzman, for
being my toughest critic and best friend.

- Drs. Eva and Heinz Wicki-Schönberg, my parents, for being
  my first role models as global citizens.

xvi

Preface

In the days after the terrorist attacks on the World Trade Center and the Pentagon on September 11, 2001—our phones were still down—I got an email message from the U.S. Military Academy at West Point. The head of the academy's Organizational Studies and Leadership department invited me to visit. It turned out that the initiative had come from the military's top brass; even the U.S. army had understood

Understanding the other side is not merely nice and morally right; it is a strategic necessity.

that in the era of globalization, its soldiers have a larger role than fighting wars. I ended up assisting the academy in the design of a curriculum to train its cadets not only as competent warriors, but also as global citizens and diplomats.

The military was not the only organization left scrambling in the aftermath of 9/11; other key agencies of the U.S. government had been caught off guard by the terrorist attacks. Why? Because Americans had lulled themselves into believing that the United States was invulnerable and invincible. They had ignored vital intelligence, become lax in their security procedures, and isolated themselves and their government from much of the world. The material and human costs have been enormous. The U.S. government has been forced to learn a whole new way of gathering intelligence on transnational terrorism—"the toughest of all intelligence targets," according to Lee Hamilton, the longtime chairman of House committees on intelligence and international relations and a member of the United States Commission on National Security. "You have to penetrate their language, their culture."[1] Understanding the other side is not merely nice and morally right; it is a strategic necessity.

> **U.S. companies must build global competencies— invest in understanding other cultures, create truly global corporate cultures, and gather competitive and human intelligence.**

But how can Americans penetrate and understand other cultures if they don't get the information? In the years since the end of the Cold War, the U.S. television networks all cut back on foreign bureaus. *Time* magazine reduced its foreign correspondent corps from 33 in 1989, to 24 in 2001—"a measure of world peace as well as of rich-world insularity," as *The Economist* put it. "A 1998 study by the University of California at San Diego found that only 2 percent of total newspaper coverage focused on world news, down from 10 percent in 1983. And network television's world coverage shrank from 45 percent of the news total in the 1970s to 13.5 percent in 1995, a 1997 study by Harvard University found. By 2001 it was down to 6 percent."[2]

Against this background of poor and parochial information, U.S. companies must build global competencies—they must invest in understanding other cultures, create truly global corporate cultures, and gather competitive and human intelligence. A cross-cultural skill-set is strategically smart and economically indispensable for both countries and government agencies to compete successfully in the global marketplace. But companies can suffer from blind spots just as much as government, media and citizens. And their blind spots can be just as costly, or more so. For example, many managers blindly assume that the 21st century is yet another American Century. But did you know that by 2007, the number one language on the Internet will no longer be English but Chinese? Did you know that by 2010, 30–40 percent of senior managers at multinationals won't be Westerners but Chinese, Indian, Indonesian or Brazilian—representing the biggest emerging consumer markets? How many U.S. or European multinationals are prepared for such global diversity? Companies that ignore these trends, or fail to respond to them, fall behind and incur huge costs in culture clashes and turf wars, post-merger pains and lawsuits, missed opportunities and brain drain. The recent multi-billion dollar losses of Coca-Cola in Europe, DaimlerChrysler's post-merger problems, and clashes between UBS and the Philippines over investment ratings are only the tip of the iceberg.

When American military planes flew over Afghanistan and dropped thousands of food packages to convince Afghans of the United States' good intentions, it was an unprecedented gesture greeted by many Afghans with enthusiasm. The only problem: the packages, assembled by a food company in Texas, contained such American favorites as peanut butter, jelly, spicy beans and rice, but standard Afghan fare consists mainly of bread, meat and rice. This endearing story is emblematic for the twin traits of the American culture: the desire to help save the world is coupled with near total ignorance of other cultures.

Similarly, many American managers don't know how to produce results in other cultures without stepping on proverbial toes and jeopardizing their missions. And let's be clear: they are not the only culprits. The ignorance can cut both ways. Executives at our European and Asian client companies tell us they don't know how to manage their U.S. subsidiaries effectively, given profoundly different management cultures. The costs on both sides can be enormous. I hope that this small book will teach managers how to minimize these costs and how to build global competencies—a crucial intangible asset in the 21st century.

TDZ, New York City, May 2003

Preface to
The Global Leader Series™

When I die I shall not be asked,
Why were you not Moses?
I shall be asked, Why were you not Zusya?
Rabbi Zusya quoted by Martin Buber[3]

Rani is an unlikely leader. From the lowly wash-
ermen's caste, scorned by the Brahmin who
have long dominated her village, she is illiterate,
30 years old and pregnant. But now Rani has
been elected to the panchayat, the village governing council, and proclaims defiantly: "I am
the boss."

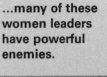

...many of these
women leaders
have powerful
enemies.

Rani lives in India, largely a rural nation.
Hers is one of 500,000 villages populated by more than 600 million people—about one in every ten people on the planet. In the
mid-1990s India passed a new law. Up to that time, for all of history, virtually all panchayat leaders had been men. But with the new
law, one-third of all panchayat leaders must be women, which has
led to the unprecedented fact that in every election one million
women are elected to panchayat leader positions. The problem is,
these women have never known how to lead or manage, how to
run an effective meeting, or how to make their voices heard. In
fact, few of them ever lift their gaze above ground when they talk
to someone. Many of them are Muslims and wear the customary
veil that shields them from exposing themselves in public.

As if that were not enough of a challenge, many of these
women leaders have powerful enemies. Alam Singh, a Brahmin

farmer who used to rule Rani's village, said angrily: "She is stupid. She is illiterate. She doesn't listen to anybody." Another peer of Singh did not leave it at angry outbursts. When a woman in his village ran to unseat him as incumbent panchayat leader, he openly threatened to kill her if she won. She won. He carried out his threat and killed her. But now her daughter decided to run for her mother's seat, won it, and is still alive and in office as of this writing.

Each of us must lead—and we must be armed with the right tools for doing so.

These courageous women stand for all people who are now summoned to lead, like it or not. As a result of the twentieth century and its revolutions, liberation struggles, and waves of democracy, more and more humans are now free to shape their own lives; not only in India, the world's largest democracy, but in most of the world. The Internet and flattened organizational hierarchies allow each of us to make an impact on our organizations and societies. With the end of the Cold War, human issues that were long suppressed by ideology have become top priorities: children (at the 1990 Children Summit), sustainable development (1992 Rio Summit), population (1994 Cairo Summit), human rights (1995 Vienna Summit), social issues (1995 Copenhagen Summit), and women's rights (1996 Women's Summit in Beijing). In this new environment, we can no longer rely on our elected leaders alone to provide leadership. Each of us must lead—and we must be armed with the right tools for doing so. Leaders like Rani lead not from above, but from below; they are co-creators, not autocrats.

The idea for this book came to me in 1996 when I prepared to leave my post as director of global operations at The Hunger Project after twelve years of service. The president of the organization asked me to write down in a "leadership manual" everything I had learned—principles, skills, methodology. On a lengthy and lonely drive home from a skiing trip, one hand on the steering wheel, the other clutching my Dictaphone, I spoke everything I knew about leadership into the little machine. I soon realized that if I were to do the assignment justice, it would take me years. So at the time I got away with writing a list. Now, half a decade later, after coaching dozens of entrepreneurs and Fortune 500 executives from Aventis to UBS, from GE Capital to GM, I can honestly say that The Hunger Project is the most skillful organization I have ever seen at managing people—or rather, at unleashing leaders to produce breakthrough results. And with the great management theorist and consultant Peter Drucker, I assert that all organizations, from firms to governments, from churches to the military, face essentially the same challenges. So it is time to make available the leadership secrets I have picked up from people like Nelson Mandela, but also from people like Rani.

But aren't there enough books on the topic already? True, there are hundreds of books talking *about* leadership; there are memoirs of great leaders that tell inspiring stories about what they did in their time; there are the seven habits and the five golden rules and the ten spiritual laws; but in my view, few (if any) books give access to leadership. Now perhaps that is too much to ask of a book, which might simply tell a great story or give useful advice. But this book attempts to be different. What you are looking at is, as much as possible, a workshop. (And what workshops nowadays are available for a sub-$20 fee?) It comes fully equipped with visuals, tips and labs (but no coffee).

As German-speaking readers know full well, my last name "Zweifel" is German for "doubt" or "uncertainty" or "skepticism." You may be wondering why someone named "Doubt," or worse, "Doubting Thomas," would write a book on leadership, since leaders are supposed to brim with confidence. But perhaps an integral element of leadership is to doubt, question, be skeptical—and not accept things at face value. Maybe leadership is based on having doubts and acting nevertheless...much as expressed by Arnold Schönberg, who famously said that courage is not the absence of fear, but action *with or despite* fear.

Speaking of doubts, let me raise some right here. My first disclaimer: if you think that this book will make something happen, you are wrong. Books rarely accomplish anything; people do, and they may or may not accomplish things by reading a book. If you want this book to be useful to you and your endeavor, you are going to have to go out into the market, into the battlefield, and actually live life. This book—any book—can at best give a framework for thinking before and between those actions. It works best if you approach it with a specific project, enterprise or relationship in mind. As my former teacher Adam Przeworski liked to say, "theories are to be used, not believed." If you don't apply this book, it might be interesting, instructive, clever; but it will remain theoretical—it will not truly affect things.

What objective is so vast that it would stretch you way beyond who you are today? (Tip: include many people in your objective.)

Take a few minutes right now and think of something you really want—an objective that you cannot achieve alone, but that requires you to lead others.

Lab

What objective is so vast that it would stretch you way beyond who you are today? (Tip: include many people in your objective.)

_____

_____

_____

What is missing in your leadership to meet this objective?

_____

What blockages (in and around you) will you need to transcend to meet the objective?

What opportunities could you take advantage of to meet the objective?

What recurring, chronic issue have you faced vis-à-vis your colleagues, buyers, or suppliers in other countries?

(I am aware that most people skip over these types of labs. But perhaps you will find it in yourself to invest a few minutes in answering these questions. What would you need to get out of it to make it a worthwhile investment of your time?)

My second disclaimer: There is not one universal, unified definition of leadership. Leadership has diverse connotations in different cultures, and most of them are misleading myths. For example, in our male-dominated culture that has prevailed for several thousand years, many people associate leadership with forceful, overbearing behavior or with command and control. Nothing could be further from the truth.

In German-speaking cultures, the word "leadership" would be translated as "Führerschaft"—not exactly a word people like to use. And Germans are not alone. Jewish scholars do "not approve of lordship, because...no mortal can lord over another... "Rabbi Johanan reportedly said, "Woe to leadership, for it buries those who possess it."[4] Both in Sweden and Japan, leadership is a much lower priority than building consensus. In Britain, "there is a degree of skepticism in the UK towards anyone who tries to lead," says the director-general of the Institute of Directors in Britain, and "a belief in the inspired amateur which discourages people from having leadership roles." This reluctance to lead is reinforced by the British view that it is unseemly to blow your own horn.

In German, the word "leadership" would be translated as "Führerschaft"— not exactly a word people like to use.

In the former Eastern Bloc countries, there is a marked reluctance to lead and take initiative, since the omnipotent state has taken charge of people's lives for so many years.

In the U.S. culture, the term leadership is used for just about anything that can be marketed and makes it sound better, from "leadership leases" to "leadership donors" or the "Democratic Leadership Council." Americans are often caught in the myth of "the faultless leader." We like to believe in Camelot, the white knight who saves us from the mundane. If our leaders are not super-human in character, we discredit and soon discard them.

Even if one unified definition of leadership were to exist, I would ask you to invent your own unique expression. As Martin Buber shows us in the motto at the head of this preface, your job is not to be like any other leader who came before you. That leader already did his or her job. Your job is to reveal your own life purpose and then fulfill that purpose with all your might.

A third disclaimer: your work with this book will be only as potent as your willingness to surrender to the book. One basic ground rule for coaches is that we do not coach someone unless they are open to coaching. Even if it were possible to coach without a demand for coaching, the results would be limited or nil, and it would certainly not be fun. So whenever you ignore certain things that the book asks of you and you don't work things through, the integrated nature of the book will be lost and you might not gain the benefits available.

Ask yourself whether you are willing to try the ideas in this book without nagging, judgment, or evaluation. Can you simply do whatever the book asks you to do? After you have worked through the book, you will have complete freedom to throw every one of them out. Try them on for now. Open yourself to the possibility that they might be useful to you.

Americans are often caught in the myth of "faultless leader."

Did you know that typical politicians spend up to 90 percent of their time preventing others from unseating them, and as little as 10 percent working for the social good they have been elected to serve? Therefore, a final disclaimer: do not use this book for harmful purposes. It offers powerful tools that can be used for building, as well as destroying, things or people. Ask yourself whether your undertaking will uplift people in some way. Unless you have that intention, or at least unless that intention is part of your endeavor, you may want to rethink your enterprise before you continue. Much misguided leadership has done much harm. Too many times, leaders have abused their power and caused damage. If you have any plans to continue this tradition, I ask you to give the book to someone else. As Gandhi said over 50 years ago, "Recall the face of the poorest and weakest man whom you may have seen, and ask yourself if the step you contemplate is going to be of any use to him. Will he gain anything by it? Will it restore him to a control over his own life and destiny? In other words, will it lead to freedom for the hungry and spiritually starving millions?"

Since you are still reading, I shall assume that you have positive intentions. As a working assumption, I believe people are driven to whatever they do either by love or by fear. All acts can be looked at as performed out of necessity. It is clear to me that such an assumption of benevolence is more often than not inaccurate, even naïve; but if I did not assume this, I would be unable to write this book. The question is: at the end of your life, what will you say about your life? What will be written on your tombstone? Will you look back upon a life of going through the motions, or upon a life of meaning, service and contribution?

At the end of your life, what will you say about your life? Will you look back upon a life of meaning and contribution?

Leadership is mysterious and unspeakable. Although I teach leadership at Columbia University, let me assure you that leadership is an art, not a science (just don't tell Columbia I said that). Perhaps leadership is akin to love: we know unequivocally whether it is present or absent, and yet it is hard to describe.

Or perhaps leadership is like fractals: the closer we look, the more confusing and the less defined it seems. Suppose someone asks you: How long is the coast of England? You might say 2,000 miles, and would be close to accurate. But this answer is only true at a level of extraordinary simplification. The closer we come to the coast of England, the more we have to take into account all the circumferences of all the little pebbles. If we go even closer, we have to measure the circumferences of grains of sand. At the microscopic level, we are shocked to discover that the answer is that the coast of England is—infinite.

Despite, or maybe because of, all these paradoxes, I trust this book will provide you with concrete tools you can use in your own quest for leadership. And hopefully it will give you something else: the courage to live leadership on a daily basis, and a bit of the courage it takes to be Rani.

Chapter One

Global Citizenship:
A Core Competence

I am a citizen, not of Athens or Greece, but of the world.
Socrates

In her 1,200-page study of Yugoslavia, Rebecca West described lying in a London hospital bed in June 1914 when she heard on the radio that a Bosnian anarchist had shot Archduke Ferdinand in Sarajevo:

> I rang for my nurse, and when she came I cried to her, "Switch on the telephone! I must speak to my husband at once. A most terrible thing has happened. The King of Yugoslavia has been assassinated." "Oh, dear!" she replied. "Did you know him?" "No," I said. "Then why," she asked, "do you think it's so terrible?"[5]

Times have changed since 1914. In the 1990s, people the world over mourned the deaths of Princess Diana and of King Hussein of Jordan instantly and intimately as if they had been family members. In 2001, millions around the world watched in horror as three hijacked planes crashed into the World Trade Center and the Pentagon. In less than a century, human beings have gone from being defined by national borders to being members of a global citizenry. Managers are part of this trend, too. In an article in *Forbes* magazine in 1998, management expert Peter Drucker declared obsolete one

Never before in history have humans dealt with humans of so many different cultures.

Extraordinary leaders—Gandhi and Churchill, Jack Welch and Bill Gates—have always lifted their gaze beyond their own borders to include the globe.

of his core assumptions: that national boundaries define the ecology of enterprise and management. Drucker defined a new reality: "Management and national boundaries are no longer congruent. The scope of management can no longer be politically defined. National boundaries will continue to be important, but as restraints on the practice of management, not in defining the practice."[6] Most managers work in a turbulent global market where one decision in Bangkok can unleash a financial crisis that affects organizations and individuals everywhere.

Globalization is both good and bad news—good because it presents us with new opportunities, and bad because it challenges our assumptions about what it means to be human today. Never before in history have humans dealt with humans of so many different cultures. Most of us meet people from other cultures every day. Even the fruit vendor on the street corner is tied up with the global market. Whether we like it or not, we are all global citizens. In this global environment, expertise in collaborating with people from different cultures will be integral to the skill-set of leaders at all levels and in all sectors of society. Leaders must embrace the whole world and our common humanity. Leadership requires taking a global perspective, synthesizing viewpoints, and collaborating across a wide spectrum of cultures. But extraordinary leaders in recent history—Gandhi and Churchill, Havel and Mandela, Kennedy and King, and also Jack Welch and Bill Gates—have always lifted their gaze beyond their own borders to include the globe.

Proposition: Building the global competencies of your enterprise requires a relatively small, high-leverage investment, but leaders who fail to make that investment early on pay an enormous price.

This book teaches the multicultural skills leaders need to succeed in any culture. It offers both serious and hilarious examples of what can go wrong when we blind ourselves to cultural differences. Through tips, exercises, and lists of do's and don'ts, you can become facile with making things happen across cultures and nations. And by the way, you need not compromise on your goals when you respect local cultures. Skillful global leaders take the appropriate cultural pathways while holding fast to their strategic intent.

The book comes in four chapters. This one discusses the new global landscape in which leaders must operate, and provides an understanding of several fundamental changes in the last generation. Chapter 2 highlights the costs of mistakes when cultures clash—and those costs can run into billions of dollars, as the cases of Coca-Cola, DaimlerChrysler and other multinationals show. The chapter then offers tools for avoiding these intercultural costs and building "global capital" in your enterprise. The chapter gives do's and don'ts in dealing with people from any culture, and excerpts guidelines written by the legendary Lawrence of Arabia for his fellow British officers in Arab lands. These guidelines are as relevant today as they were in Sir Lawrence's day, and most of them are applicable to any culture not our own. Chapter 3 covers cross-border alliances as the acid test of global citizenship and gives case studies of successful mergers and acquisitions—for example GE Capital's integration model, which the company learned in the action of integrating over 100 acquisitions. Chapter 4 is about the nuts and bolts of preparing and leading global meetings successfully.

A Global Citizen's Mini-Briefing

What an extraordinary situation is that of us mortals.
Each of us is here for a brief sojourn for what purpose
he knows not, though he sometimes thinks he feels it.
But from the point of view of daily life,
without going deeper, we exist for our fellow men.
In the first place, for those on whose smiles and welfare
all our happiness depend
And in the next place, for all those unknown to us personally
with whose destiny we are bound up.
A hundred times a day, I remind myself that my inner and outer life
depend on the labors of other men living and dead.
And that I must exert myself in order to give in th
same measure as I have received and am still receiving.

Albert Einstein

A participant in one of our programs, Jim May of Dow Corning, told me a term executives and workers use in his company: the "idiot factor" means that the farther away people are from us, the more we think of them as idiots. (The "idiot factor" is at work not only in culture clashes, but also between divisions, for example Sales vs. Product Development, or technical vs. non-technical people.) You should assume that the idiot factor is at work always and anywhere, whether you are conscious of it or not. One way to counteract the idiot factor is to see the world as a whole and the connections between things, as well as how others live around the world— essential vistas for leaders. Sometimes statistics can give us a picture of the world like nothing else can:[7]

> The "idiot factor" means that the farther away people are from us, the more we think of them as idiots.

- World population: 6,137,000,000.
- Births per 1,000 population: 22. Deaths per 1,000 population: 9. Natural annual increase: 1.3 percent.
- Projected population in 2025: 7,818,000,000; in 2050: 9,036,000,000.
- Infant mortality rate (= infant deaths per 1,000 live births):

56. Highest IMR in the world: Angola (198 per 1,000), followed by Afghanistan (154 per 1,000). Lowest IMR: Andorra (1 per 1,000).

Shrink the world's population to a village of 100 people—6 people would possess 59% of the entire world's wealth.

- Humans under 15 years of age: 30 percent (in Africa, 43 percent). Humans over 65 years old: 7 percent (in Africa, 3 percent).
- Secondary school enrollment: 58 percent of males, 50 percent of females.
- Number of women who die annually from pregnancy-related causes: 585,000 (1 per minute).
- Percentage of world food produced by women: 70 percent.
- Per-capita Gross National Product worldwide: $4,740 per year (in Eastern Africa $210).
- Percentage of the world's resources owned by the wealthiest quintile (20 percent of the world's population): 84 percent. Percentage owned by the poorest quintile: 1.7 percent.
- Number of United Nations employees: 53,589. Number of employees at Disney World and Disneyland: 50,000.
- United Nations peacekeeping expenditures: $2.63 billion (approved), $3-3.5 billion (projected need). World military spending (1995): $798 billion.

Another, perhaps even starker, way of looking at the world is to imagine that we can shrink its population to a village of 100 people, with all the existing human ratios remaining the same.[8] Here is how such a village would look (approximately):

- 57 would be Asians, 21 Europeans, 14 from the Western hemisphere (both north and south), 8 Africans.
- 52 would be female and 48 male; 89 would be heterosexual and 11 homosexual.
- 70 would be "of color" and 30 white, 70 would be non-Christian and 30 Christian.
- 6 people would possess 59 percent of the entire world's wealth, and all 6 would be from the United States.

- 80 would live in substandard housing.
- 70 would be unable to read.
- 50 would suffer from malnutrition.
- 1 would be near death; 1 near birth.
- 1 would have a college education.
- 1 would own a computer.

When one considers our world from such a compressed perspective, the need for understanding and education becomes glaringly apparent. If you awoke this morning with more health than illness, you are better off than the one million people who will not survive this week. If you have never experienced the danger of battle, the loneliness of imprisonment, the agony of torture, or the pangs of starvation, you are ahead of 500 million people in the world. If you can attend a church meeting without fear of harassment, arrest, torture, or death, you are more blessed than three billion people in the world. If you have food in the refrigerator, clothes on your back, a roof overhead and a place to sleep, you are richer than 75 percent of the world population. If you have money in the bank, in your wallet, and spare change in a dish somewhere, you are among the wealthiest 8 percent of the world's people. And if you can read this book (a pretty safe assumption), you are more advantaged than two billion people in the world who cannot read.

Lab

This exercise is designed to acquaint you with how about one-quarter of humanity lives. All you need is a few moments and your imagination. Imagine yourself in your own house. Now take the television(s) out. Take away the refrigerator and freezer, the stove, the dishwasher, the microwave, the washing machine and dryer, the burglar alarm, and all other appliances. Instead you have a small wood stove for cooking and heat. Now take away the heat. Take away safe drinking water. Take away your bed. Take away the other furniture. Take away electricity; you have candles. Take away all carpets; you have an earthen floor. Take away the bathroom; you have to go outside to relieve yourself, and you wash yourself from a bucket of water. Now take away your house; you have a shack or hut with one room and a corrugated tin roof. When the sun shines, it gets unbearably hot. When it rains, the roof leaks and all your possessions get damp.

If you have money in the bank, in your wallet, and spare change in a dish somewhere, you are among the wealthiest 8 percent of the world's people.

Now imagine that you are a woman. You have five children and are pregnant again. You have had four years of schooling, more than most girls in your community. You get up before dawn to walk 20 miles to the neighboring village to get water and matches for the stove. The nearest school is there too. The nearest doctor is 50 miles away in an overfilled clinic.[9]

The New Landscape:
Global Is In, National Is Out

> *We aren't passengers on Spaceship Earth, we're the crew.*
> *We aren't residents on this planet, we're citizens.*
> *The difference in both cases is responsibility.*
> Rusty Schweikert, Astronaut

Now that we have embraced our world and seen our own culture in comparative perspective, we turn to globalization, a new label for a fact older than nations. The nation-state has been the norm and primary actor in international relations only since 1648—the Peace of Westphalia—while transnational organizations existed many centuries ago. Take the Roman Empire and the Catholic Church. Rome was a multicultural, multi-ethnic imperial super-state that spanned several continents. The Church, especially before the Lutheran and Zwinglian Reformations, was a super-state that commanded immense economic might and capital assets, military strength for crusades, cultural and ideological power, and enormous manpower. Church agents were an influence in virtually every kingdom, fiefdom and township.

For much of history, only a tiny elite ever traveled more than walking distance from where they were born.

But since World War II, several factors have transformed our experience of our global identity. For much of history, only a tiny elite ever traveled more than walking distance from where they were born. Now the average person has a sense of the nearness of other lands and the world as a whole. The factors that have brought about this transformation include:

- the decrease of communication costs and transportation costs; the increase of international migration, and the emergence of the virtual team;
- the breakdown of world Communism, the rise of global media and the Americanization of global culture;
- the rise of international organizations and multinational corporations, and the end of industry specificity.

These transformations have made a global orientation essential for today's leaders. We briefly examine each.

Communication, transportation, migration, virtual teams. The Internet and the deregulation of telecoms have dramatically reduced the cost of long-distance communication. Exchanging information with people almost anywhere in the world has become easier, faster and cheaper than it ever was for previous generations. (Note, though, that the overwhelming majority of the global population does not benefit from these lower costs. According to Intel, 2 billion people in the world have never made a phone call in their lives.[10] 26 percent of Americans use the Web, but only 3 percent of Russians, 0.2 percent of Arab states' populations and 0.04 percent of South Asians do so. An

American needs to save one month's salary to buy a computer; a Bangladeshi must save all his wages for eight years to do so.[11]

Because distance is no longer an obstacle, relationships once difficult to maintain are now commonplace. I regularly call clients in Europe and Australia from New York City for 11 cents a minute, or e–mail them messages, documents or entire books for the price of a local call. (The book you are reading right now is an example of this development.)

One American telecommunications company is taking advantage of low rates by using customer service reps in Bangalore, India who pose as Americans with American names, trained to speak in American accents with American customers. "Hi, my name is Susan Sanders, and I'm from Chicago," a 22-year-old introduces herself with a broad smile and even broader vowels. In fact, "Susan Sanders" is C.R. Suman, a native of Bangalore who fields calls from customers in the United States. Just in case her callers ask personal questions, Ms. Suman has created a fictional biography, complete with her parents Bob and Ann, brother Mark and a made-up business degree from the University of Illinois. Her training by Customer Assets, the calling center, included listening to sit-coms like "Ally McBeal" or "Friends" without the picture and then reconstructing the dialogue, and being quizzed by the trainer, who would pose as a caller, on American movies, sports and television programs. The point of the pretense is to convince Americans that the person on the other end of the line works right nearby—not 8,300 miles away. Companies like General Electric or British Airways have set up supermarket-sized phone banks in cities like Bangalore or Haiderabad to handle a huge volume of daily customer inquiries. India is attractive because of its widespread use of English and its low-cost labor.

> One American company is taking advantage of low rates by using customer service reps in India who pose as Americans.

Indian call-centers serving United States customers are only the low end of a huge and growing industry of cross-border virtual teams: Indian software developers, transcribers, accountants, web designers, and animation artists. "India is on its way to being the back office for the world," says Shriram Ramdas, co-founder of Bangalore Labs, which manages web sites and information networks for companies from the outskirts of Bangalore. While their American clients sleep, Indian software writers churn out code, which is then beamed by satellite to the United States. According to McKinsey & Company, this industry will spawn 800,000 new jobs and $17 billion in revenue by 2008. Subroto Bagchi, a partner in a software firm, says: "We see ourselves as a next-generation company that is neither Indian nor American."[12]

Transportation is also easier and cheaper today than ever before. In 1900, traveling from New York City to London took usually six days and cost a fortune. Today, a flight from New York to London takes seven hours and as little as $180. Needless to say, many more people are now able to travel, and those who do travel much farther and more often than they did in the past.

Lower transportation costs enhance international mobility and migration. According to one estimate, there were 100 million migrants in the world in 1992—roughly one out of every fifty humans.[13] Swiss friends tell me that in some parts of Basel or Zurich, up to 80 percent of students in primary schools are now from abroad—from countries like Bosnia, Turkey, Lebanon, Senegal— because of Switzerland's relatively liberal immigration policy. People migrate for many reasons: to flee political repression, escape poverty, seek economic opportunity or join loved ones.

Global capitalism, world media and Americanization. The breakdown of the former Communist states has compounded the Americanization of global culture. With the exception of China, Cuba, North Korea and Vietnam, the world has embraced capitalism (which is seeping even into these countries) and pushed many millions of new consumers and producers into the global economy. There is now one Western model of consumption, for better or for worse. Influenced by Hollywood films that reach all the corners of the world, by Western-style advertising, by CNN and MTV, people the world over tend to have more and more uniform tastes. They access AOL, smoke Marlboros, listen to Red Hot Chili Peppers, and watch Seinfeld. Even in Bulgaria, J.R. of "Dallas" fame is a revered icon on billboards. The unprecedented concentration of world media in the hands of just a few—Rupert Murdoch, AOL/Time Warner, and the BBC—certainly compounds this growing uniformity of tastes.

Multinational corporations, international organizations. World capitalism is coupled with yet another transformation: the rise of global corporations. Multinationals per se are not a new phenomenon. Fiat, General Motors, and several European insurance companies were already multinational entities in the nineteenth century.

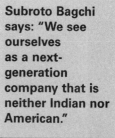

Subroto Bagchi says: "We see ourselves as a next-generation company that is neither Indian nor American."

What is new is their stunning growth in recent decades. If the most prominent example, Microsoft, were a country, it would be the ninth-largest economy (in terms of Gross Domestic Product) in the world. The annual sales of GM are now larger than the GDPs of Thailand or Norway. Ford generates more income than Saudi Arabia. The national identity of multinationals can be a confusing matter, since production processes too have become global. The "Japanese" company Toyota is one of the larger employers in the United States. It produces cars with American workers, American management, and American parts. Should Toyota still be seen as a Japanese firm? Mabuchi Motor controls half the world market in mini-motors for zoom lenses, toothbrushes, and car windows, and employs 33,000 workers, only 1,000 of whom live in Japan. Over 40 percent of the market for Coca-Cola, Gillette, Lucent, Boeing, and GE power systems is in Asia.[14] Even the stalwart American company General Motors produces 40 percent of its cars beyond American shores. The company is as multinational as each of its cars. Whether GM is still an American firm is doubtful.[15]

Given their global infrastructure and marketing, companies need truly global management. Diversity is becoming a fact of life within the top management teams of multinational corporations. In their *Harvard Business Review* article, "The End of Corporate Imperialism," C. K. Prahalad and Kenneth Lieberthal predict that by 2010, over one-third of board members of multinationals will be people from China, India, Indonesia and Brazil, since those countries will be the most populated and fastest-growing markets. The authors assert that businesses will run into troubles unless they diversify their management early on.[16]

The emergence of international institutions in the second half of the 20th century also had a profound effect on globalization. The General Agreement on Tariffs and Trade and its successor, the World Trade Organization, lowered trade barriers around the world. World trade increased from $308 billion in 1950 to $3.5 trillion in 1995 (although growth slowed almost to a halt in 2001, when trade grew by only 2 percent). The World Bank and the International Monetary Fund dictate economic policies in Turkey, Tajikistan and Togo. The European Union is rapidly becoming a regulatory super-state with its own currency and central bank, courts and legislature, flag and (soon) army. This proliferation of international organizations, and the delegation of more and more competencies to them, has led some to claim that the days of the nation-state are numbered.

The flow of information, people, goods and money around the world ($3 trillion move around the world each day) has accelerated to such an extent that it seems as though the world has shrunk; and by seemingly shrinking the world, super-fast communication and transportation have altered our experience of time, which seems to be speeding up. Some call this phenomenon Internet time: one Internet year equals four months. When the American colonies proclaimed their Declaration of Independence from Great Britain, it took several weeks for the news to reach England. It now happens instantaneously. When the United

States-led coalition declared war on Iraq in 1991, Saddam Hussein reportedly watched the event live on CNN.

Globalization can be good news if it leads to better understanding and greater harmony among cultures. Or it can be bad if local tastes or preferences are obliterated in favor of super-brands like MTV, Madonna and McDonald's that dominate by virtue of their superior marketing muscle; or if we have become interconnected to such a degree that European and American investors tremble at economic developments in Thailand, Japan, or Brazil. For better or worse, we now live in a world in which the proverbial butterfly that flaps its wings in Bangkok can in fact unleash a storm in California.

Toyota is one of the larger employers in the United States. It produces cars with American Workers. Should Toyota be seen as a Japanese firm?

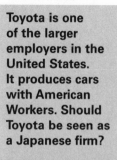

Some argue that the globalization trend is countered by opposite trends.[17] In response to the growing homogenization of humanity, they point to growing nationalism, ethnic division, and "tribalism" that hold many areas of the world in their grip. Others argue that at the very time when barriers to communication, travel and trade have come down and we make contact with more people in more places, we feel less and less connected. They say that the concept of the "individual," which was a powerful invention in the eighteenth century, is getting out of hand; the cult of individualism and the free market have led to diminished relationships and to isolation—to a "you or me" world. As powerful as these counter trends are, they do not alter the direction in which we are heading—toward globalism.

We cannot deny that coordinating activities worldwide is much more complex for firms than managing within the same nation. Managing an empire around the world brings seemingly insurmountable issues of a cultural, political, technical or communicative nature. Non-tariff barriers, standards and laws impede commerce between countries, and state subsidies of certain

This proliferation of international organizations... has led some to claim that the days of the nation-state are numbered.

industries make competition difficult. There are national differences—different tastes or languages, different media or practices. Cultures may have different speeds: the rhythm of a typical Swedish movie is much slower than that of an American movie, but way too fast for Indian viewers. The rhythm of an Indian movie is so slow that you learn meditating just by watching. (This example is not trivial: if global companies want to reach the key markets of the 21st century, the growing Indian middle class is a larger audience than the entire population of the United States or even Europe.)

What Is Your Cross-Cultural IQ?

Cross-cultural, cross-functional and multilingual knowledge and fluency will be among the most highly valued assets in the emerging managerial landscape, whether one works in a global, regional or national organization.

Mary O'Hara-Devereaux and Robert Johansen,
Institute for the Future

If globalization is such a unifying force, why do we have to care about local cultures when almost everyone in the world today drinks Coke, wears Levi's or a Swatch, and works on Windows or Apple?

Not so, however. Not only do tastes differ (teenage boys in Botswana might discuss cows with the same passion that U.S. teenagers reserve for sports cars), but the very patterns of thought are culturally based, too. Although philosophers and psychologists have assumed for more than a century that the same basic processes underlie all human thought—a penchant for rationality, categorization and linear thinking in terms of cause and effect—

they are now finding that the very patterns of thinking vary from culture to culture because they are culturally constructed. "We used to think that everybody uses categories in the same way, that logic plays the same kind of role for everyone in the understanding of everyday life, that memory, perception, rule application and so on are the same," said Dr. Richard Nisbett, a social psychologist at the University of Michigan. He and his colleagues found that people not only think about different things; they think differently: "We're now arguing that cognitive processes are just far more malleable than mainstream psychology assumed." Dr. Nisbett's study, conducted in the United States, Japan, China and Korea, found that Easterners appear to think more "holistically," to pay more attention to context and relationships, rely more on experience than on abstract logic and show more tolerance for contradiction.

For example, asked to analyze a conflict between mothers and daughters, American test subjects quickly sided with one or the other, while Chinese subjects tended to see merit on both sides, commenting for example that "Both the mothers and the daughters have failed to understand each other."

The growing Indian middle class is a larger audience than the entire population of the United States or even Europe.

In one study, students from Japan and the United States were asked to comment on an animated underwater scene in which one large fish swam among smaller fish and other aquatic life. Japanese subjects made 70 percent more statements about the background environment than did Americans, and twice as many statements about the relationships between animate and inanimate objects. "Americans were much more likely to zero in on the biggest fish, the brightest object, the fish moving the fastest," Dr. Nisbett said. "That's where the money is as far as they are concerned." The bottom line: culture matters regardless of globalization.

Cultural differences are not written into the genes: for example, many Asian-Americans born in the United States are indistinguishable in their thought patterns from European-Americans. But if history is an indicator, fundamental cultural differences will stay around for a long time. Occidental thinking has existed at least since ancient Greece, favoring adversarial debate, logical

Easterners appear to think more "holistically", to pay more attention to context and relationships.

argument and analytic deduction. In China, meanwhile, an appreciation for complexity, context, and the "yin and yang" of life was cultivated for many centuries.[18]

Lab

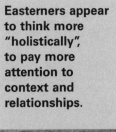

Observe your own global citizenship. Make it a practice to remember the common humanity of all people when you ride the subway, drive to work or watch television. See the cultures, the colors, the creeds, the customs. Feel the planet under your feet when you walk.

Whether we like it or not, global citizenship is in, parochialism is out. Being merely a national citizen is passé. Being a global citizen is not merely a fad—it is also necessary for our survival as a species. Most major issues of our time transcend national borders: AIDS, war and the arms trade, environmental destruction, poverty, debt crises and transnational terrorism. Unless we are able to transcend those borders as well, we have no hope of dealing successfully with the world we live in.

Lab

When you read the paper, read it as a global citizen. Learn about the global citizenry: how do most people around the world live? Open an atlas to a page at random and obtain information about how people live there.

Be a global citizen in all your actions and all your thinking. Live as though each of your actions had an impact somewhere on the planet —it probably does. We are interconnected, and our connections are increasing.

Before we go to Chapter 2, I would like you to do a quick multiple-choice exercise. (Sorry, but exercises *are* good for you.) It is called "What is your cross-cultural IQ?" Check the right answer for each statement:

A. Generally, Swiss businesspeople, relative to Americans, like:
1. thicker, more detailed legal contracts
2. thinner, less detailed legal contracts
3. contracts with the same level of detail

B. A Singaporean colleague invites you to his home for dinner. It is appropriate:
1. to bring wine
2. to bring baked goods or fruit for the whole family
3. to bring four flowers

Many Asian-Americans born in the United States are indistinguishable in their thought patterns from European-Americans.

C. In meetings, Germans generally prefer, compared to Americans:
1. a more structured agenda
2. a less structured agenda
3. the same level of structure

D. Eastern Europeans, in general, compared to Western Europeans, show:
1. more leadership and initiative
2. less leadership and initiative
3. about the same level of leadership and initiative

E. Compared to American businesspeople, Japanese business-people:
1. take longer to build consensus because they give each team member a chance to comment
2. take less time to build consensus because leaders impose their views

     3. take about the same time to build consensus because both 1 and 2 are true

F. Americans are seen by other cultures to be mainly:
1. individualist and moralist
2. capitalist and short-termist
3. both 1 and 2

Chapter Two

Preventing the High Costs of Culture Clash

In the Austrian army of the nineteenth century, officers expressed their familiarity by addressing each other with the familiar *Du* form of "you" used elsewhere only for friends or servants, rather than the more formal *Sie* normally used in German-speaking society. In World War I, when Austria allied itself with Germany, German officers felt themselves being insulted or, worse, propositioned by their Austrian colleagues who addressed them with the intimate *Du*.

Colgate introduced a toothpaste in France called "Cue", the name of a notorious pornographic magazine.

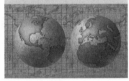

Such cultural misunderstandings continue to this day. Here are some more current examples of hilarious mistakes when cultures collide:[19]

- Chevrolet introduced its Chevy Nova model in the Latin American market, but was puzzled to find virtually no demand. Too late, the company found out that "Nova" was understood as *no va,* "does not work."

- Coors put its slogan "Turn it loose" into Spanish, where it was read as something like "Suffer from diarrhea."

- Clairol introduced the "Mist Stick," a curling iron, into German only to find out that "mist" is slang for manure. Few customers had use for the "manure stick."

- The American slogan for Salem cigarettes, "Salem— Feeling Free", was translated for the Japanese market as "When smoking Salem, you will feel so refreshed that your mind seems to be free and empty."

- When Gerber started selling baby food in Africa, it used the same packaging as in the US, with the baby on the label. Only later did the Swiss company learn that since most people in Africa don't read English, companies routinely put pictures on the label of what is *inside* the container.

- Colgate introduced a toothpaste in France called "Cue", the name of a notorious pornographic magazine.

- An American T-shirt maker in Miami printed shirts for the Spanish market to promote the Pope's visit. Instead of "I saw the Pope" *(el Papa),* the shirts read "I saw the potato" *(la papa).*

- In Italy, a campaign for Schweppes Tonic Water translated the name into "Schweppes Toilet Water."

- Coca Cola's "Coke Adds Life" slogan translated into Chinese, came out as "Coke brings your ancestors back from the grave."

- Frank Perdue's chicken slogan "it takes a tough man to make a tender chicken" was translated into Spanish as "it takes an aroused man to make a chicken affectionate."

- When Parker Pen marketed a ballpoint pen in Mexico, its ads were supposed to have read, "it won't leak in your pocket and embarrass you." Instead, the company thought that the word *embarazar* (to impregnate) meant to embarrass, so the ad read: "It won't leak in your pocket and make you pregnant."

- The U.S. Dairy Board ran into problems when it tried to translate its widely promoted Got Milk campaign for the Hispanic market. "Got Milk?" in Spanish is *¿Tienes Leche?,* which means "Are you lactating?"

- The Scandinavian vacuum manufacturer Electrolux used as its slogan in an American campaign: "Nothing sucks like an Electrolux."

The 10 Most Costly Sins When Cultures Clash

But often the consequences of cultural misunderstanding are no laughing matter—less funny but more expensive. The costs can run into billions of dollars. Motorola's flameout was one of the more spectacular. The company deployed its Iridium global satellite system to offer truly global telephone service, but its global strategy was out of touch with the global realities. The company was too enamored of its global vision that it did not take time to gauge local demand before building its hugely expensive satellite infrastructure. And there was not enough demand, to say the least. When Iridium was shut down, its sunk cost to Motorola was $3.5 billion. But that is just the tip of the iceberg. Here are the ten most costly sins companies commit when doing business in other cultures:

> **When Iridium was shut down, its sunk cost to Motorola was $3.5 billion. But that is just the tip of the iceberg.**

Sin #1: You think the world plays by your rules. We have already seen that few places anywhere are unaffected by Americanization. U.S. companies represented 95 percent of the stock market value last year. Almost anywhere, people buy from Amazon, listen to Bruce Springsteen, eat "begols" in Paris or at Dunkin' Donuts in Rome. For many Americans, the United States is evidently the whole world. Less than 15 percent of them even own a passport. (A valiant exception is the management consulting firm McKinsey. In 1980, 36 percent of the company's senior partners were outside the United States; by 1994, 52 percent. In 1994, the 148 senior partners elected Rajat Gupta, an unassuming 45-year-old from New Delhi who was born in Copenhagen, as managing director. Mr. Gupta's selection reflects the growing influence of non-Americans: McKinsey's leaders clearly felt that the company needed a global citizen and consensus builder at its helm.)

In the 1990s the U.S. management model of unfettered capitalism—free markets, free agents, deregulation, low taxes, individual accountability, management by objectives—was hailed as the underpinnings of economic growth anywhere in the world. The European and Japanese model of the welfare state and social responsibility seemed a relic of the past. But now, according to the Global Competitiveness Report for 2000, the most competitive nation worldwide is no longer the United States but Finland, a welfare state par excellence. Apart from the number two spot held by the United States, the top eight are all European countries. France, for example, has a host of regulations protecting the rights of employees. Its entrepreneurial track record is limited, and it was never a particularly enthusiastic convert to the Anglo–American model of the free agent. Indeed, the French retain a liking for bureaucracy, August vacations, long lunches, and leaving the office at five. Only 10 percent of French full-time workers work more than 46 hours per week. The French government introduced a 35-hour workweek in 1999. A study carried out by *Fortune* magazine in 2000 found that it took six minutes to register a new business in California, but six weeks in France. Yet despite all this, the French economy was doing rather well. Unemployment had fallen below 10 percent. At that time, employment expansion was faster in France than in the United States.[20] American managers could learn something from Europeans—for example, the ability to manage diversity and multiculturalism in a multilingual European Union.

> **In 2000, the most competitive nation worldwide is no longer the United States but Finland, a welfare state par excellence.**

Consider Nokia, the Finnish company that used to make diapers. Nokia now holds the global lead in smart phones, which may become the dominant point of access to the Internet. Nokia and other European companies may well drive U.S. competitors out of the market. Why? Nokia rallied around GSM (Global System for Mobile Communications), a common European standard, while U.S. companies keep competing with a handful of incompatible standards.

On the other hand, take Coca-Cola, for which Europe of late has been a desert without refreshment in sight. The company learned the hard way that the rest of the world is not simply an extension of the United States. In 1999 the Italian Antitrust Authority fined Coke more than $16 million for keeping competitors out through illegal discounts, bonuses and exclusive deals with wholesalers and retailers, since in Europe the threshold for "dominant position" can be as low as 40 percent, while under the U.S. Sherman

The very thing that had always been its success formula now cost the beverage giant multi-billion dollar losses in sales.

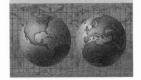

Antitrust Act, monopoly power requires well over 50 percent market share. The company also found itself under scrutiny for taking undue advantage of its near-monopoly when European regulators scaled back Coke's acquisition of Cadbury Schweppes' non-U.S. beverage business from $1.85 billion to $1.1 billion. French courts rebuffed its coveted purchase of the best-known French soda brand, Orangina.

Sin #2: You do what you always did in the past. But the biggest blow came when some 250 people in Belgium and France became sick with nausea, abdominal pains, vomiting, and diarrhea from drinking a contaminated Coca-Cola shipment. The company did what it had always done: it insisted—with characteristic American optimism—that all was well, and failed to educate the European public. The result: several governments ordered Coke off the shelves. These calamities could have easily been prevented by creating a truly global corporate culture and by building some basic cross-cultural skills for top managers at the company's Atlanta headquarters. The very thing that had always been its success formula now cost the beverage giant multi-billion dollar losses in sales, a huge setback in public relations, and a plunge in shareholder value.

...language is the house of being. It reflects cultural essence.

Coca-Cola has learned from that calamity. In 2001, it collaborated with the French govern-ment and voluntarily recalled bottles in danger of contamination. More importantly, Coke now aspires to respect diversity and local leaders. "You can't apply a global standard of measure-ment to consumers," Coke's new chairman and CEO Douglas Daft says, "because it reduces everything to the lowest common denominator." Daft knows about cross-cultural skills: an Australian, he rose through the ranks for 30 years and was long based in Asia. Virtually a stranger in the Atlanta head-quarters when he succeeded Douglas Ivester, Daft swiftly decen-tralized decision-making to the local level and began embracing local brands and flavors.

Sin #3: You take English for granted. True, English is the #1 world language and is even encroaching on the turf of other languages. In Germany, English is the most widely studied foreign language in schools, and a mixed language called "Denglisch" is becoming more and more fashionable. Audi promises you "die power." Lufthansa's slogan is "Thinking in new directions." Volkswagen launched the "New Beetle." "New Beetle sounds more hip than neue Käfer," said Sabina Metzner of Volkswagen. "We wanted to make clear that the Beetle might have some resem-blances to the old Käfer, but it is very much a modern car."

Not everybody is thrilled. A professor of economics at the University of Dortmund was so disgusted with the "spineless con-formity" of Denglisch that he founded the Society for the Protection of the German Language and instituted an annual booby prize for the "Sprachpanscher" ("language diluter") of the year. In 1998 alone membership soared from 200 to 4,000.[21]

But isn't it simpler if we all speak the same language world-wide? "Of course managers can communicate in English," says Porsche's chairman Wendelin Wiedeking. "But that is not the case on all work levels. It gets quite difficult when it's about details, for example engine parts. But precisely in these matters, workers must understand each other perfectly."[22]

And language is not just about communication. As the German philosopher Martin Heidegger wrote, language is the house of being. It reflects cultural essence. Sony's founder Akio Morita, who became one of the best loved Japanese people in the West, gave a great example. He once said in a TV interview that when Westerners "ask questions or express an opinion, they want to know right away whether the other party agrees or opposes them. So in English, 'yes' or 'no' comes first. We Japanese prefer to save the 'yes' or 'no' for last. Particularly when the answer is 'no,' we put off saying that as long as possible, and they find that exasperating." Morita created a private club for business leaders whose motto was inscribed above the bar: "We Japanese businessmen must be amphibians. We must survive in water and on land," in the incompatible worlds of East and West.[23]

The Chinese version of Windows 95 was programmed to display references to "communist bandits."

Sin #4: You don't respect the cultural pathways for making things happen. Some American multinationals are on the defensive in Europe because of simple *faux pas* in their cross-cultural business dealings. When Disney built its EuroDisney theme park in Paris, it triggered a visceral hate campaign among the Paris intelligentsia, and angry French people boycotted EuroDisney en masse. The company had tailored the theme park on its U.S. parks model. Practices that made sense in the United States enraged the French: EuroDisney's kiosks failed to serve the wine and local food that French people love. Disney's

> I decided to meet with the deputy and launch into work immediately. It was the biggest mistake I ever made.

screening process for job applicants was an affront to accepted socialist beliefs in France. The company's calamities inspired ridicule. A trendy French magazine compared the long-term impact of EuroDisney to that of a nuclear bomb and listed the radioactive fallout at point zero, at ten miles from point zero, at fifty miles, and so forth. It took Disney years and a new (French) company president to make basic adjustments, restore its image, and meet EuroDisney's profitability goals. Small wonder that fist-swinging farmers achieved the status of résistance heroes by throwing tomatoes at McDonald's facilities.

Other companies can step on regulatory toes. In late 2000 a French court ordered Yahoo to bar French citizens from purchasing Nazi memorabilia on its web site. From a French legal perspective, the case was clear: Yahoo was breaking the law. In the United States, the case was equally clear: the French ruling amounted to censorship and violated the First Amendment. Both perspectives are right, depending on where you stand. It goes to show how profoundly culture and customs shape the reality you see.

Sin #5: You don't stand in your host's shoes. And Yahoo was not alone. A report commissioned by the French defense ministry accused Microsoft of using its systems to spy for the CIA. But while Microsoft could shrug off the allegation by France, China dealt it a more serious blow. The Chinese version of Microsoft's Windows 95 was programmed to display references to "communist bandits" and to exhort users to "take back the mainland." Microsoft had made one mistake: it had used programmers in Taiwan to write the software. Furious with Microsoft, the Chinese government decided to back Linux instead—a decision potentially disastrous for Microsoft in a country that has become the third-largest software market in the world.[24] (In October 2001 Microsoft closed a high-profile deal with Samsung to compensate for the calamity.)

Another example is one of the largest U.S. banks, which frankly behaved like an American bull in a European china shop. They were launching a new set of policies in Europe and forgot to ask their European colleagues what they thought. Europeans don't like that. They like to co-create; they like to be consulted. After our intervention, the U.S. middle managers started listening and the conference became a success. But before that, the bank's people in New York were wondering why the Europeans did not return their calls. The Europeans basically stopped interacting with global headquarters, since they were under the impression that headquarters was unwilling to see the world from their point of view.

Sin #6: You forget to invest in relationships. Executives at a New York-based Fortune 500 investment bank complained bitterly that their European counterparts completely ignored their communications. After some prodding I found that the Americans had never bothered to create partnerships with the Europeans. They would call London or Frankfurt just before end of business GMT and tell people, "I need this report on my desk today." Not a good idea.

It is easy to talk about other people's mistakes, but I made plenty of my own. I learned about the value of relationship-building the hard and painful way in 1987 during a four-month assignment in India. The managing director of the organization I was to work with was out of town when I arrived. She had sent her deputy to meet me at the airport. In my youthful impatience, rather than wait for the managing director to return, I decided to meet with the deputy and launch into work immediately. It was the biggest mistake I ever made. Not only did I fail to create the relationship and trust necessary to conduct business effectively, but I also imposed my will on my host country. The managing director, feeling that I had bypassed her authority, mistrusted me from the start and attempted to undermine my efforts. She, and many of my Indian colleagues, saw me as an intruder who was meddling with their operation. I ultimately got the job done, but my impatience and insensitivity had thrown an unnecessary wrench into my own project.

I later learned from a colleague of mine, who had been on a similar assignment, that he had been much more circumspect. When he had arrived in India, there had been no meetings, no reception, not a phone call from the people with whom he had come to work. This had gone on for two weeks, he told me. He had kept himself busy reading, settling in to his apartment, and learning about the culture. After two weeks, the managing director finally called him and asked, "What do you want?" He replied, "Let's meet and see what *you* want." He was ready to work, and made clear that he had come to be of service, rather than imposing himself and his agenda, in Western fashion, as I did. His work had been successful, and graceful.

Another factor would also have made a difference in my trip: more conscious preparation. My trip had been set up on a short and perfunctory conference call. A senior executive at global headquarters announced to the managing director in India that I would come there to work. Confronted with that news, the managing director said the polite thing to say in India: "Great!" I discovered later that she had never endorsed the trip. What I should have done before going was call to find out what she wanted and to build, or verify, a demand for my services. My visit was doomed before I ever got on the plane.

In 1990, when I was based indefinitely in Japan (but ended up staying only seven months), I made sure not to make the same mistake again. I verified through several conference calls with the CEO of the organization in Tokyo that he indeed had a high demand for my coaching, and I kept a low profile until I had built a sufficient base of relationship. (A fun side effect: I drank a lot of sake with my Japanese colleagues and investors—the socializing glue of drinking is virtually the only accepted avenue for Japanese executives to get acquainted with one another). Like Coke's Daft, I came to appreciate the value of relationships and "face time."

Well, actually it didn't go all that smoothly either. After I arrived, the management of the host organization gave me a gorgeous apartment in a Tokyo high-rise—with an incredible view, a table shaped like a baby-grand piano, a great video and sound system. I felt like a king. After about two-and-a-half weeks, I was told quietly but in no uncertain terms that I'd "better move out." I said, "No problem. When?" "Today." "Today?" My grace period had come to an abrupt end. I had nowhere to go. I ended up finding a tiny apartment in the printer's district. Had I done anything to deserve such brusque treatment? I will never know. That is part of the mystery of living in Japan. You never know if you just made a mistake or even committed a capital sin, because you may not find out for 10 years, if ever.

The women pointed at my body hair and giggled. I figured they had probably never worked on a Westerner before.

It took me months to recreate the relationship and reestablish my credibility (assuming I had ever had it). I listened a lot. I was in innumerable meetings where I stayed silent and attentive, seeking to be part of the consensus. One day a major shift happened. The CEO invited me to accompany him to the bathhouse. That was how he conveyed to me that he was ready to take our relationship to the next level. I felt like being knighted. I was elated—until I stepped up to the hot tub, that is. The water was so hot that I could almost not bear getting in; the CEO chuckled as I got into the steamy water. Afterwards, he and I lay on massage tables as 60-year-old stocky women performed a kind of dance on our backs. The women pointed at my body hair and giggled; I figured they had probably never worked on a Westerner before. I must have seemed like a nice monkey to them. But the bottom line was that the CEO had graced me with his invitation. From then on, I was his partner (no small feat, given that even today some Japanese university libraries still carry books that "prove" the inferiority of the Western brain compared to the Japanese brain).

...I learned how important it is to keep hold of your strategic intent while taking the appropriate cultural pathways to achieve that intent.

Although it had seemed terribly inefficient to a Westerner, my careful relationship-building paid off in the end. He and I produced extraordinary financial results together. (He even suggested at one point that I should marry a Japanese woman and settle there...)

Unpleasant surprises are the rule in unfamiliar cultural settings. I will never forget the lunches I had with my friend Mikio Uekusa, the owner and president of Akebono Inc. and a key investor, at company headquarters—particularly the first one. Uekusa-san's personal secretary brought us each a black, lacquered box containing our lunch. The box was beautiful, but the contents were not. I peaked inside and shivered at the sight of the jello-like, milky, translucent mass. Forcing a broad smile on my face, I used the elegant wooden chopsticks to take a piece of one of the blubbery masses. It tasted awful. My smile disappeared, but I tried to put it back on. I discreetly looked for a plant to spit the food into, but no plants were in sight. What to do? If I wanted Uekusa-san to place the calls I had asked him to make to other $100,000 investors, I knew I had to enjoy the food that he so generously provided. (Reminiscing about these lunches much later, I came to think that Uekusa-san must have been testing me, and probably laughed his head off behind my back.) After lunch, I pulled out my investor list, dialed the phone, and handed the receiver to Uekusa-san, all with nauseous vengeance. Virtually every call produced a $100,000 investor. Later that afternoon, we drove around in his black Mercedes to pick up the money from the investors.

I learned two lessons from this experience. The first is obvious: when in Rome, do as the Romans do. Second, and more importantly, I learned how important it is to keep hold of your strategic intent while taking the appropriate cultural pathways to achieve that intent. You must be committed to your strategic intent, yet you also must be flexible about doing whatever the particular culture demands. It may not be a straight shot. It may feel as though you are wasting time, particularly if you are a Westerner, because you will not be doing what you would in your own culture.

> In Europe, the How—the bridge between vision and action—must be crystal clear to people before they take action.

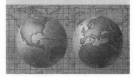

My work in Japan required a deep investment in relationships and socializing, doing strange things and going to unfamiliar places. Coupled with a steadfast commitment to the end goal, the investment paid off.

Sin #7: You jump from vision to action. But I had no time to rest on my laurels. The year's end was fast approaching, and neither the Europeans nor the Americans came through with their funding commitments to global headquarters. On one of our global executive team calls, the chief operating officer at the time decided to override my objections and come to Tokyo with his three most trusted lieutenants to bail the global office out. They arrived sometime in December, which left a ridiculously short timeline before Christmas and the New Year to fill a multi-million dollar hole in the global budget. The Japanese said that they did not really see the usefulness of such an intervention, but that they trusted the global office leadership. We tried to mobilize the Tokyo staff to produce a financial miracle. The attempt failed miserably, and the fundamental trust that our Japanese partners

One "victim" of this "storming of the village" told her that this was the "exact same thing the Russians did—just no tanks."

had for the global office was shattered. This happened in 1990, and to this day I do not know whether the Japanese have forgiven the global headquarters for going in without creating a shared strategy. For years and years afterwards, even though I was director of global operations, the Japanese subsidiary refused my requests or feigned not understanding them. Our relationship was cordial on the surface, but had become testy and reserved underneath. If I brought up the subject of money head-on, I might lose the entire relationship; if I tip-toed around the issue, I had no money. So I ended up with neither.

The lesson: unlike in Japan, Nike's credo "Just Do It" reigns supreme in the United States. "Just Do It" in this case translated into "Let's just go to Japan," implying that we would somehow find the way through once we were on the ground. But reliance on learning-by-doing can backfire in a culture that values strategy. Managers must put in the other building blocks of accomplishment—relationship, vision, strategy—before taking action. This is true not only for Japan: in Central and Northern Europe, for example, the How—the bridge between vision and action—must be crystal clear to people, preferably in writing, before they take action.

Sin #8: You take the village by storm. Unfortunately American companies seldom recognize this. A colleague told me that when General Electric launched a new initiative in Hungary, the Americans in charge got off the plane, did a dog-and-pony show of GE core values, and left. One victim of this "storming of the village" told her that this was the "exact same thing the Russians did—just no tanks."

Another example: one American investment banker sought to buy a private bank in Switzerland. When he arrived for a first exploratory meeting with the bank's owners in the small town where they lived, he opened the meeting by saying that his train would leave very soon, and asked that they get down to business. The owners just smiled politely and said good-bye. Of course it never came to a second meeting, let alone a transaction.

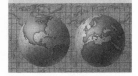

Though touting DaimlerChrysler as a "merger of equals," Europeans dominated the new entity from the start.

Let me balance out the impression that U.S. multinationals are the only culprits, though. It takes two to tango, and many a cross-cultural gaffe originates in Europe. Without the least bit of *Schadenfreude* (an untranslatable German word for glee at the damage of others), I recall my prediction in a speech in mid-1999 that the merger of Mercedes and Chrysler would fall on its face. The writing was on the wall: just ten months after the merger that created DaimlerChrysler, the American top executive in charge of integrating the operations in Stuttgart with those in Auburn Hills resigned. Though touting DaimlerChrysler as a "merger of equals," Europeans dominated the new entity from the start. Co-chairman Jürgen Schrempp put himself firmly in charge, pushed all but two Americans from the management board of the combined company and installed his trusted German aide Dieter Zetsche at Chrysler's helm. DaimlerChrysler paid dearly for this new brand of German imperialism: at the time of this writing, the company's revenue was to fall by 13 percent and operating profits as much as 75 percent in 2001, forcing it to eliminate 26,000 jobs and suffer major brain drain from the loss of some of Chrysler's most creative talent.

Sin #9: You select the wrong people. Then again, managers may have put the right people in the wrong expatriate jobs to begin with. All too often, senior managers move executives to a target country based on their technical skills alone, rather than also on their cross-cultural expertise; or they get the mix of expats and local leaders wrong. "We don't do a very good job of selecting people for foreign postings," concedes Sir Brian Pitman, chairman of Lloyds Group PLC. The British bank sent a brilliant young executive to Argentina. "He only lasted one week," Pitman said. "He just didn't fit in."

Sin #10: You forget that your advice is noise in their ears. The final high-cost mistake you can make is to fail to build a demand for your words. To use the DaimlerChrysler case once more: already the first joint board meeting of the merged company was a disaster. Former CEO Robert Eaton told a journalist: "Germans have a penchant for coming to meetings armed with tons of overhead transparencies and colored charts. It's an absolute information overkill."[25] The German managers had not taken care to adjust their presentation to American cultural expectations and had instead blindly rolled out their program.

Respect people, their ideas and their cultures. Be polite, on your best behavior, not loud.

I committed a similar mistake when I was based in India. It took me months to realize that I was dispensing unsolicited advice. And when there is no demand for it, even your best advice turns into noise pollution. A few weeks into my assignment, it dawned upon me that telling people what to do made no difference; what was needed was not giving answers but asking questions and listening. Most people in most places have a good reason, at least subjectively, for doing what they do. Barging in and imposing changes is of course always possible, but should be used only as a last resort. Your efforts will meet with resistance unless you can create a demand for your intervention and end up with people as owners of the changes they need to make. Even in the change-happy United States, where many see change as an adventure, resistance can be high. So how would you react if an executive from Switzerland or Japan came in and told you how to run things?

But even when expatriates fit in beautifully with their host culture, a common mistake multinationals make is that they don't listen to their expats when they return. According to a survey by the Center for Global Assignments, 61 percent of employees who returned from overseas postings said they lacked opportunities to put their experience abroad to work at home. Every year, thousands of executives arrive home from overseas assignments, only to leave their jobs in the hope of finding greener pastures, often at a sunk cost of $1 million or more that their employer invested in training and overseas expenses. 25 percent leave within a year— and typically go over to the competition. In one extreme case, a company lost every one of 25 managers it had sent on international assignments within one year of their return. Cost: $50 million.[26]

How to Avoid Culture Clashes

Are there solutions? There are. Danone SA reduced its failure rate among expat managers from 35 percent to 3 percent in the three years since it started using a relocation assessment program. Motorola learned from its mistakes, too: the company now uses a workplace simulation program to identify and evaluate its international managers.

Resist the urge to immediately resolve issues— hearing them is often enough to dissolve them.

General Electric used to be an American company working internationally, treating the world outside the United States simply as an export market. But that is changing: the day is not far off when GE will earn more outside the United States than domestically. GE needs to build global skills. Jack Welch, the former chairman and CEO of General Electric and one of the most revered business leaders of our times, recognized this several years before his retirement in a speech to GE executives:

> The Jack Welch of the future cannot be like me. I spent my entire career in the United States. The next head of General Electric will be somebody who spent time in Bombay, in Hong Kong, in Buenos Aires. We have to send our best and

greatest overseas and make sure they have the training that will allow them to be the global leaders who will make G.E. flourish in the future.

GE backs these words with action. New hires at GE's Crotonville training center are given crash courses in global issues. Senior executives are routinely sent on 4-week trips to foreign markets, then returned to Crotonville to brief top executives. The intention is to build what Welch calls a multipolar and multicultural company.

But how do you build multicultural skills? I suggest three tools: rules of conduct; decoding a culture; and a tool we call "Global Results Pyramid™."

Tool 1: Do's and Taboos of Global Citizenship

The first tool is a set of guidelines for global citizens. They sensitize you and your colleagues to the Do's and Taboos, the unwritten rules of conduct when working across cultures.

- **Watch your hosts** and do what they do. For example, American-style sporting analogies ("slam dunk," "cover all bases," or "step up to the plate") are unlikely to be understood—avoid them.

- **Never take English for granted.** Remember that if English is not your business partners' first language, they accommodate you with every English sentence they speak or hear.

- **Respect** people, their ideas and their cultures. Be polite, on your best behavior, not loud.

- **Interact with people as individuals,** not as culture. Resist the urge to generalize.

- **Listen** when people tell you all their issues. Listening is a vastly underrated skill. Resist the urge to immediately resolve the issues—hearing them is often enough to dissolve them.

- **Be open** to input and to learning. You can learn enormously from other cultures (both about them and yourself). If you feel that you know a culture already, that there is nothing new, you will be right. There will indeed be nothing to learn. Assume you don't know.

- Remember that understanding even one country or culture can be a **quest of a lifetime**. It is not something you can check off and be done with.

- Say so if you don't know. **Don't wing it.**

- **Find the gate** to the village if it is fenced in. Do not take the village by storm.

- **Talk to someone who is clear** whenever you are not clear. Keep a shared understanding with your partners on your mission. For example, check in on a weekly basis with your superior or partner back at headquarters—somebody who can help you step back from the challenges and make sense of them.

- **Remember that your advice is noise** in their ears unless they want it.

- **Follow up** on promises and agreements. "I heard you say the package would be here by 3pm and it is not. I am puzzled." Do not accuse, do not get upset, but inquire until you are satisfied.

- **Roll with the punches** if you are sabotaged. Free yourself from the attachment to a particular picture or form. There may be another pathway to your goal than the one you had in mind.

- **Know that you _will_ make mistakes**; the question is how to recover. (It was Nelson Mandela who said that "The greatest glory of leading lies not in never falling but in rising every time you fall.")

- And don't forget when you greet a member of the opposite sex: one kiss in the United States, two in Britain and most of Europe, three in Switzerland, four in France...

Tool 2: Decoding Culture

The second tool trains your muscle of decoding a culture (be it of a corporation or a country). You can distinguish three layers of culture.[27] The most apparent are the visible and audible signs and behaviors you can readily observe: language, logos, dress codes,

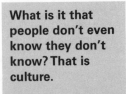

What is it that people don't even know they don't know? That is culture.

architecture, movies or styles. The second layer is how people justify and rationalize the first layer: "The way we do things around here is...because..." The third and innermost layer is what I understand as culture: the past decisions that have become so automatic as to become invisible, even unconscious. What is it that people don't even know they don't know? That is culture.

Now, how do you decode this innermost, invisible culture? An elegant way involves three facets. The first is to understand the ideology and values of the *founders*. The myth of William Tell, who ambushed the Hapsburg vassal Gessler and catalyzed a movement to throw out the Hapsburgs and found Switzerland, is telling if we want to understand why Switzerland jealously guards its neutrality, and has steadfastly refused to join the United Nations or the European Union. The founders of the United States enshrined their values of life, liberty and the pursuit of happiness, which are underpinnings of U.S. culture (by contrast, no European constitution contains such a fundamental right to pursue happiness). To understand Israel, you would want to learn about David Ben Gurion and Golda Meir. Learning about them would tell you a lot about the Israeli culture.

Another facet in decoding a culture is to see who are the *outcasts*—in other words, what behaviors are not permissible, even taboo, in the dominant culture. For example, when I was in Cuba I saw how the Latin machismo culture, including the state, oppresses and ridicules homosexuals. In the U.S. culture, atheism is permissible, but atheists find themselves clearly outside the mainstream and are suspect to the mainstream. It is virtually impossible for atheists to run for political office.

The third step is to look through the history of a culture and identify wars and other (for instance, economic) crises that are often *defining moments* in shaping a culture. The First and Second World Wars helped shape the self-understanding of U.S. culture that America is always the good guy fighting against the bad guys to save the world. Wilson declared that the U.S. was fighting World War I to "make the world safe for democracy." By its entry into World War II, the U.S. prevented Nazi Germany's world dominance. Both wars ended the Monroe Doctrine which had mandated that the U.S. stay out of meddling in European affairs. But by 1944, the U.S. actively espoused a new role—that of saving the world (from Nazism, then from Communism, and most recently from terrorism). From then on, the U.S. saw itself as a benevolent hegemon, imposing democracy in Germany and Japan, going to war in Korea and Vietnam and the Persian Gulf, underwriting much of the UN system, monitoring elections in Zambia, etc. "We know what is good for the world" has become an unquestioned assumption not only in U.S. foreign policy, but also in U.S. multinationals.

But of course these three facets—founders, outcasts, defining moments—are not the only way to decode a culture. Before you do business in another country, here are several key areas you will want to understand, ideally before you go, or at the least after you get there:

- **Economy.** Determine the engines of the country's or region's economy. What are the most important sectors? How dependent is the economy on outside sources and trade? Imports and exports account for only 9 percent of the GDP of the United States, compared to 20 percent of the GDP of the Netherlands. Its greater dependence on external trade makes the Netherlands much more open to other cultures than is the U.S.

- **History.** Identify key formative events, factors, and actors in the culture's history and economic development (historic leaders, wars, revolutions, and economic crises). Identify the importance of foreign influences. For instance, if you want to understand Switzerland, you would have to understand that Switzerland has safeguarded its neutrality since 1815, has not had a war since 1848, and had its last general strike in 1919. These events have helped shape an aversion of Swiss people to conflict.

> The United States has a strong antitrust culture and a belief in the value of competition, while most European countries long believed in cartels.

- **Geography.** Look at a map of the country. Is it locked in by natural borders or exposed? What are its immediate neighbors? What are its natural resources? Japan and Britain are island nations. This has arguably contributed to their aloofness from their respective continents (the United Kingdom being reluctant to join the EU, Japan having strained relations with its East Asian neighbors).

- **Religions.** What is the country's dominant religion? What principles does that religion teach? What behaviors does it proscribe? What, according to the dominant religion, are the obligations of the individual and the community? Catholicism in France and Italy provides absolution from sins, and in so doing encourages a *joie de vivre.*

- **Government.** If the society is governed by a constitution, read it (most national constitutions are posted on the Web). What is the authority of government institutions and of political parties? What role does government play vis-à-vis companies, trade and foreign influence? For example, the United States has a strong antitrust culture and a belief in the value of competition, while most European countries long believed in cartels as a tool of economic statecraft, and have come to espouse anti-cartel laws only recently.

- **Attitude to outsiders.** Are there many immigrants in the culture? Is the country rather open to them or rather closed?

- **Media.** Who in the country has access to world media like CNN or BBC? How many people have access to the Internet? In Kenya, a small elite in government and academia accesses the Web, while the general population depends on the radio for news and weather forecasts. Which media are the most widely circulated? Americans watch TV the most, while Russians and Germans have the highest newspaper readership.

- **Education.** Determine the country's literacy rate and the value and mode of learning and training. How important is educational background for credibility in business? In France, virtually all members of the business elite have been groomed for leadership in the Grandes Ecoles (Great Schools). In the U.S., you can be a revered entrepreneur without so much as a college degree.

The Global Results Pyramid™ has helped our clients maximize global results and navigate pitfalls in cross-cultural projects.

- **Mobility.** How mobile are people in the U.S.? Mobility is very high and people tend to be willing to move more often to advance, while in Switzerland people tend to stay in their hometown all their lives and stay loyal to the same employer. My father worked for Sandoz—later Novartis—for 35 years and stayed in Basel his entire professional life.

- **Population.** Find out the size of the population and income distribution. Is there a large and strong middle class? How many people live below the subsistence minimum? Who are the elite? In most sub-Saharan African countries there is barely a middle class. In Germany, the elites are the church, the written word, and academia, so clergy members and intellectuals have disproportionate power to shape public opinion, whereas in the U.S. businesspeople have much more power and status. (Donald Trump running for president would be unthinkable in Germany.)

- **Language.** What is the dominant language, and what other languages are spoken in the country? Are minority languages accepted and encouraged by the majority? Switzerland has established four national languages, and three of them are official languages in which all government business is conducted. In 1848, Switzerland decided against a prime minister, and instead adopted a seven-member collective executive to give minorities a voice in governing.

- **Popular myths.** Who are the heroes of the culture? Why? What qualities do these heroes embody for people? How are these values reflected in day-to-day business? Israeli national leaders often come from the army or Mosad (the secret service): Yitzhak Rabin, Ehud Barak and Ariel Sharon are only a few examples of the prestige the military enjoys in Israel. And many Israeli businesspeople are used to being among the most combative negotiators in the world.

Tool 3: The Global Results Pyramid™

The third tool in avoiding culture clash is the Global Results Pyramid™ below. It is a simple model for: 1) producing results in a cross-cultural environment; 2) preventing cross-cultural mistakes in executing projects; and 3) troubleshooting once mistakes happen. To build any successful accomplishment, you need to make sure that four levels are fulfilled: relationship, vision, strategy, action. The Global Results Pyramid™ has helped our clients maximize global results, navigate pitfalls, and minimize costs in cross-cultural projects.

A disclaimer is in order here: any model of reality simplifies reality. Many of the characterizations of cultures that follow are flagrant generalizations. Of course there are always exceptions to the rule. But generalizations can be very useful. In fact, generalization is the essence of culture: enough people act or think in a certain way to make that way of living a general tendency. But please remember that cultures are only tendencies, and the Global Results Pyramid™ only approximates reality, it can never fully reflect reality.

Building Global Results

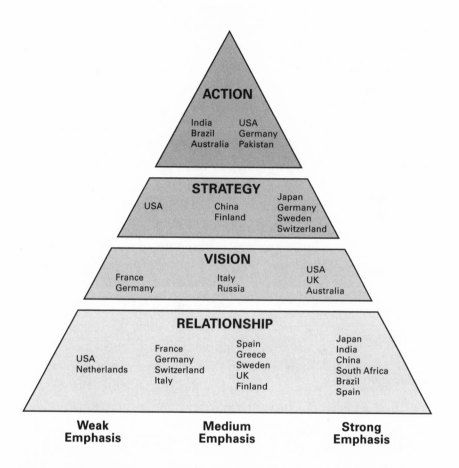

Figure 1: Global Results Pyramid™. © 2001 Swiss Consulting Group

In order to produce an accomplishment of size, a project must move through four stages: relationship, vision, strategy, and action. Different cultures emphasize these levels differently. If managers fail to respect the cultural emphasis on a particular level, cultures will inevitably clash.

[Note: Countries are chosen as illustrations only, and represent approximations of real situations.]

Relationship. The first level of the pyramid is relationship—and that is true in any culture in the world, but in some much more than in others. In some cultures, such as the United States, relationship is much less important than in other cultures, such as Japan or Chile or Saudi Arabia. You remember my war stories above, when I lived in India and Japan. For example, when the chief executive of my client invited me to accompany him to the bathhouse, it was a big breakthrough in our relationship. It was very important for him to develop the relationship and trust between us before getting down to business. In Western cultures, by contrast, people downplay or simply ignore relationship-building. They go beyond the relationship quickly, to vision or strategy or worse, directly to action. They are so hungry for results that they forget that relationship—including partnership, team spirit, shared values and trust—is the foundation for all accomplishment. If you can deepen and broaden the foundation of your relationship with others, you can increase the height of the pyramid you can build. In other words, the deeper the relationship, the greater the possible accomplishment. At this ground level of the Pyramid, you ask, "Who are we?"

Many Europeans have a tendency to be skeptical of vision (no wonder, given their long history of grand visions that ended disastrously).

Vision. Once you have a deep enough relationship, the next level of the pyramid is vision. What is the bigger picture that you and I are committed to? Before you have that shared vision, delving into strategy or action is risky because you and your colleagues will not pull in the same direction, or your strategy will simply be an extension of the past into the future rather than emanating from the future. At the Vision level you ask: "What are we here for?"

One culture that is quite visionary is the one in the United States. Americans in general tend to be optimistic about the future. They see a new future as an adventure and are open to creating an outlandish vision. Another culture that tends to be enamored with vision (as opposed to action to implement vision) is the British. If you negotiate with Britons, you might find that they like to keep brainstorming and exploring, and are reluctant to go into strategy or action. They love to flirt and hate to...jump into bed.

Many continental Europeans have a tendency to be skeptical of vision (no wonder, given their long history of grand visions that ended disastrously). While Americans tend to commit the mistake of jumping from vision to action, Europeans tend to make another mistake: they jump from vision to strategy too quickly by asking "But how do we do this? I can't see that this can be done." The German head of an American company's European subsidiary went to a global meeting where his American bosses and peers advocated the vision of increasing profits from $300 million to $1 billion within a year, an admittedly ambitious if not outlandish goal. The German managing director could not see the strategy and immediately nixed the project without allowing a full, uncensored conversation of possibilities.

Strategy. The third level of the pyramid is strategy. Once you have built the partnership and a common future that all key stakeholders are committed to, you then must build the strategy to make your vision a reality. It is at this point that you ask, "How do we get there?" You deal with people's concerns about how to do it, what to do if something does not work, and what could go wrong. Only when you have the strategy do you go into action, the top level.

How do you create ownership in the strategy? Include key leaders from all subsidiaries or affiliates in meetings to create strategy and policies, or to align on other decisions that will affect their operations. Begin these meetings by achieving a shared understanding, and stay with it until an abiding consensus has been reached. This alignment will allow you to operate effectively

> In Switzerland and Germany, Nike's slogan "Just Do It" doesn't do it. They want to think things through and then take action.

for one year (or less in a fast-changing industry). Be sensitive to when the next meeting is needed to create the strategy, policies, and agreements for the next cycle. In between these meetings, use occasional conference calls, or videoconferences, to sustain the relationship and handle any issues that arise. Be willing to invest in co-creation with your affiliates. The investment may seem expensive, even nerve-racking, but the return is handsome. I did this when I was director of global operations for The Hunger Project, and global affiliates increased revenue by 500 percent in five years while holding expenses stable, once we had created an environment of shared partnership, vision and strategy.

Action. As we saw above, one mistake Americans often make is to jump into action too quickly. Before the relationship is clear and the strategy is created, they want to launch into action. They are confident that action will provide learning-by-doing. They like to "Just Do It." In addition, they tend to manage by objectives and often have urgent deadlines to meet. They have to produce the results by the end of the quarter or the week. But going into action too quickly robs people of a fuller understanding of the whole strategy. People in some countries such as Germany and Switzerland must understand how they are going to get things done before they go into action. As long as they are not convinced that the How is clear enough, they often resist getting into action. In Switzerland and Germany, Nike's slogan "Just Do It" doesn't do it. They want to think things through and then take action. That way of being can, of course, lead to other pitfalls. Germans may get so attached to a certain action or set of procedures that they cannot stop what they are doing, even if it is strategically wrong or does not work anymore. The same

German president above was known for sticking with well-established pathways and opposing innovative ideas that had yet to be proven valid.

You can use the Global Results Pyramid™ for troubleshooting in action. If people are upset, for instance, you can make a safe bet that relationship is insufficient or missing altogether. If people are not clear about the future and skeptical, even resigned about the future, and if they think "This is the same as it ever was," that is when a common, inspiring vision is missing. If people are undecided or confused, if they don't know what to do, or if they have a lot of concerns, strategy is missing. And finally, if people fail to keep their agreements, what's missing is action, in particular specificity about the action and clear deadlines. But often, a lack of action is the symptom of the fact that other floors of the pyramid are built shoddily, or missing altogether. For example, if there is a lack of compliance in global subsidiaries, the people involved probably never owned the strategy in the first place. Go back to how the strategy or policy originated. Did the subsidiaries or affiliates have a voice in its shaping? Were they clear on the rationale (or purpose or vision) behind it? Or were they simply expected to adopt and abide by it? And, before the strategy, do people own the vision underlying the strategy? Is it a common future, or is it the vision of only a few executives in a closed boardroom at global headquarters?

> "Go easy just for the first few weeks. A bad start is difficult to atone for...."
>
> **Lawrence of Arabia**

Lawrence of Arabia—A Global Citizen of His Time

These differences of emphasis on relationship, vision, strategy and action and the culture clashes they breed are far from novel. They probably have plagued cross-cultural enterprises ever since humans began to deal with other cultures. One early global citizen living in and adapting to another culture and documenting his cross-cultural lessons was T.E. Lawrence, the legendary "Lawrence of Arabia." Lawrence wrote his *Twenty-Seven Articles*[28] for British officers stationed in Arab countries. We need to treat his writing with caution: he represented the interests of the British Empire, and his *Articles* are sometimes racist, often arrogant and condescending, and always filled with generalizations. His prejudices show Lawrence clearly as a member of his ruling class and a man of his time. Nevertheless, taken out of that specific context, we can gain from his words some indispensable guidelines for dealing with any new culture. When I lived in India, for example, I committed some of the very errors Lawrence warns against—you have seen my war stories above—and was forced to learn my lessons the hard way. Had I had the benefit of the *Articles,* my conduct would likely have been more circumspect and would have saved me from several costly fiascos. I give you below a taste of Lawrence's wisdom.

> The following notes have been expressed in commandment form for greater clarity and to save words. They are however only my personal conclusions, arrived at gradually while I worked in the Hedjaz and now put on paper as stalking horses for beginners [...] They are of course not suitable to any other person's need, or applicable unchanged in any particular situation.

> 1. Go easy just for the first few weeks. A bad start is difficult to atone for....

> 2. Learn all you can....Do all this by listening and by indirect inquiry. Do not ask questions. Get to speak their [language], not yours. Until you can understand their allusions avoid getting deep into conversation, or you will drop bricks. Be a little stiff at first.

> 3. In matters of business deal only with the commander of the Army, column, or party in which you serve. Never

give orders to anyone at all, and reserve your directions or advice for the C.O., however great the temptation (for efficiency's sake) of dealing direct with his underlings. Your place is advisory, and your advice is due to the commander alone....

4. Win and keep the confidence of your leader. Strengthen his prestige at your expense before others when you can. Never refuse or quash schemes he may put forward: but ensure that they are put forward in the first instance privately to you. Always approve them, and after praise modify them insensibly, causing the suggestions to come from him....

5. Remain in touch with your leader as constantly and unobtrusively as you can. Live with him, that at meal times and at audiences you may be naturally with him in his tent. Formal visits to give advice are not so good as the constant dropping of ideas in casual talk....

6. Your ideal position is when you are present and not noticed. Do not be too intimate, too prominent, or too earnest....

7. ...However friendly and informal the treatment of yourself may be, remember always that your foundations are very sandy ones....

8. Cling tight to your sense of humor. You will need it every day. A dry irony is the most useful type, and repartee of a personal and not too broad character will double your influence with the Chiefs. Reproof if wrapped up in some smiling form will carry further and last longer than the most violent speech....

9. Never lay hands on an Arab—you degrade yourself. You may think the resultant obvious increase of outward respect a gain to you: but what you have really done is to build a wall between you and their inner selves.

10. ...The less apparent your interferences the more you influence....

11. Religious discussions will be fairly frequent. Say what you like about your own side, and avoid criticism of theirs....

12. The open reason that Bedu give you for action or inaction may be true, but always there will be better reasons left for you to divine. You must find these inner reasons (they will be denied, but are none the less in operation) before shaping your arguments for one course or others. Allusion is more effective than logical exposition: they dislike concise expression. Their minds work just as ours do, but on different premises....

13. ...Avoid too free talk about women. It is as difficult a subject as religion, and their standards are so unlike our own, that a remark harmless in English may appear as unrestrained to them, as some of their statements would look to us, if translated literally....

14. The beginning and ending of the secret... is unremitting study of them. Keep always on your guard; never say an inconsidered thing, or do an unnecessary thing; watch yourself and your companions all the time; hear all that passes, search out what is going on beneath the surface, read their characters, discover their tastes...and you realize your part deeply enough to avoid the little slips that would undo the work of weeks. Your success will be just proportioned to the amount of mental effort you devote to it.

Chapter Three

Alliances and M&A: The Acid Test

All men are caught in an inescapable network of mutuality,
tied in a single garment of destiny.
Whatever affects one affects all indirectly...
I can never be what I ought to be until you are what you ought to be,
and you can never be what you ought to be until I am what I ought to be.
This is the interrelated structure of reality.

Martin Luther King, Jr.

Now that we have some tools for maximizing cross-cultural results and minimizing the costs, we can apply our knowledge to an area where cross-cultural failures happen most often: alliances, mergers, acquisitions, and joint ventures. Statistics tell us that more than half of attempted mergers and acquisitions fail; the number might even be higher with cross-border alliances. According to alliance consultant Larraine Segil, "Cross-border alliances are among the most challenging of alliance relationships—taking at least two to three times longer to create versus a domestic alliance." Segil

Neither company conducted a full needs analysis to understand the other side's primary agenda.

researched 200 companies in 60 industries and found that 75 percent of companies surveyed believed that alliance failure was caused by incompatibility of country or corporate cultures.[29] It is hardly necessary to cite examples:

- I already mentioned DaimlerChrysler above, where the German Daimler executives are now dominating virtually every key position in the combined entity, while Chrysler

51

people have little if any say in the leadership of DaimlerChrysler.

- A much older example, one of the first, is the failed joint venture of AT&T and Olivetti in the mid-1980s. The American and the Italian company attempted a partnership for their computer and word processing products, with Olivetti manufacturing the products and AT&T marketing and selling them under the AT&T brand. Tapas Sen, a former senior AT&T executive, told me that "we didn't quite understand what it takes to do business with another culture. First, our team was not conversant in the Italian language, so we always depended on their understanding of English." But language was only one of the barriers to understanding. Neither company conducted a full needs analysis to understand the other side's primary agenda; and the companies never quite clarified their mutual expectations with each other. The Italian Olivetti culture was massively different from AT&T's culture. The two companies did not get along and finally had to agree to get a divorce.

- When BMW merged with Rover, German managers opted for a hands-off management style for fear of stepping on the toes of their British counterparts. (Germans are typically seen as command-and-control managers in Europe.) That was the wrong move. The merger failed famously when BMW was forced to sell the Rover Group after posting billions of dollars in losses.

- A Swedish-American pharmaceutical company reportedly might run into a lawsuit because senior managers in the U.S. reportedly withheld information from their Swedish executives when they asked them to move to New Jersey. The company promised each Swede a Green Card, when in fact they never intended to grant people resident status.

- Below we will review GE Capital's integration model as a useful method for integrating acquisitions. But even GE is not exempt from cross-cultural mistakes in mergers. Jack Welch's autocratic and aggressive style in the negotiations with the EU Competition Authority was one of the causes of the GE/Honeywell merger's prohibition and failure, wrote Michael Bonsignore, the former chief of Honeywell in the *Financial Times*. In particular, Welch's wrathful behavior vis-à-vis Competition Commissioner Mario Monti "was a case study in how not to handle process and protocol."[30]

These are just a few examples of what can happen in mergers when cultures collide. When things work fine, alliances are wonderful. The question is, what do you do when there is a breakdown? Will you hold the line of the alliance, or will you default to some old behavior that worked once in the past but is now obsolete?

In mergers and acquisitions, the same principles apply as in relationships: people tend to do to others the things they expect others to do to them. One problem is that we rarely express exactly what we expect. We avoid figuring out just what we want, when, how often, and from whom; and if we do, we do not tell the other party, get a shared understanding, or follow up if the other party does not meet our implicit

> ...people tend to do to others the things they expect others to do to them. One problem is that we rarely express exactly what we expect.

standards. The other problem, in business-to-business relationships and negotiations just as in personal relationships, is the failure to stand in the shoes of the other party. All too often, leaders apply different standards to themselves, depending on their role in a particular business relationship; they are not willing to give their suppliers the trust they expect when they themselves are suppliers. If you are engaged in a M&A yourself, or if you manage any relationships with buyers and/or suppliers, I want you to do another small exercise (yes, they are still good for you):

Lab

Unexpressed expectations are deleterious to relationships or alliances. Pick one of your key alliance partners or contractors, current or

53

potential. Then, first, answer the following questions: What are your specific expectations of your alliance partner or contractor? What do you count on them for? What can they count on you for? Given your answers to these questions, what are your biggest questions still unanswered?

Second, do something that actors do routinely: try to stand in their shoes and embody them. This requires a great deal of empathy on your part. Try seeing what their specific expectations are of you. What is most important to them? What can they count on you for? Given the answers to these questions, what are their biggest questions still unanswered?

The GE Capital Model of Integration[31]

Between 1993 and 1998 alone, GE Capital integrated more than 100 mergers, increasing its workforce by 30 percent, globalizing

[GE Capital managers] regard integration as a full-time job.

its business and doubling its net income. The company sees integration management as a separate business function, just like operations, marketing or finance. GE seeks to address cultural issues head-on by using "Cultural Workouts" managed by outside facilitators to speed up integration and foster understanding of the partner company's culture.

The GE Capital model of integration includes seven steps that its managers take whenever the company merges with another firm:

1. They look at integration as a process—not as a science, but as an art. Even though there are predictable elements, we will never fully understand what it takes to work with other human beings.

2. They make use of cultural assessment tools. The executives meet for several days, usually with an outside consultant, and identify the cultural barriers that the merging entities face.

3. They regard integration as a full-time job, and they allocate a manager to monitor the integration effort full-time until it is complete.

...it is essential to communicate, communicate, communicate.

4. They use urgency to catalyze immediate results, by designing what I call a catalytic project for the teams to work on together. This is a small-scale, short-term project— usually lasting no more than 100 days—on which the teams can work together. There are several advantages in using a catalytic project: the teams can learn how to work together in an environment that is easy to control; any breakdowns can be resolved right away; and producing immediate results gives people a sense of success.

5. They recognize that it is essential to communicate, communicate, communicate. You should never assume anything. You have to communicate powerfully and instantaneously if there is any possibility of a misunderstanding.

6. They use three-day cultural workouts to train people in multi-cultural skills. The purpose of these sessions is to enable people to understand each other. They learn about each other's history and culture, the war stories of each company, what people are proud of, and what they do not like about their company. In this way, they build relationship and partnership. The cultural workout is usually scheduled for the last three days of the 100-day project. It forges the two companies as a team. On the last day, they create the future together. They create a vision and a strategy and agree on the actions they will take together in the future.

7. They use a facilitator or coach. This could be a coach from within one of the merging companies, but it usually works better if

he or she is outside the two cultures. That way the coach can bring a fresh point of view and see more impartially what drives these people and what their cultural blind spots are.

Tool 4: Global Integrator™

The previous chapter covered three tools for avoiding cross-cultural gaffes. The spider graph in the box on the following page can

You can map the two cultures onto each other so that you can see the similarities and discrepancies.

help you understand the culture of your M&A or JV partner. You can map the two cultures onto each other so that you can see the similarities and discrepancies. I have assigned a scale of 0 to 10 to each of eight dimensions; each should be seen as a continuum. The dimensions overlap, of course. In the graph, I have pitted the U.S. culture against that of France for illustration purposes. (The same disclaimer as above applies: all dimensions and ratings are generalizations and only approximate reality.)

Global Integrator

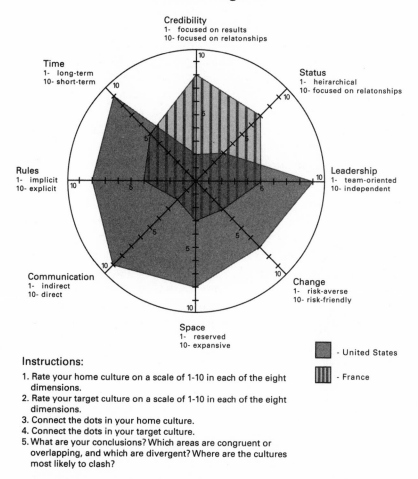

Credibility
1- focused on results
10- focused on relatonships

Time
1- long-term
10- short-term

Status
1- heirarchical
10- focused on relatonships

Rules
1- implicit
10- explicit

Leadership
1- team-oriented
10- independent

Communication
1- indirect
10- direct

Change
1- risk-averse
10- risk-friendly

Space
1- reserved
10- expansive

■ - United States

▥ - France

Instructions:

1. Rate your home culture on a scale of 1-10 in each of the eight dimensions.
2. Rate your target culture on a scale of 1-10 in each of the eight dimensions.
3. Connect the dots in your home culture.
4. Connect the dots in your target culture.
5. What are your conclusions? Which areas are congruent or overlapping, and which are divergent? Where are the cultures most likely to clash?

Figure 2: Global Integrator™. © 2001 Swiss Consulting Group

- **Credibility** (focus on results—focus on relationships). How do people gain or lose credibility in the culture? How measurable are accomplishments in people's work? How does a person's past performance influence that person's future or career prospects? How important is prior relationship for business? What is more important, achievement or connections? French colleagues tell me that in

57

their country, it is generally less important what you know than whom you know. No matter what your track record, you can secure a top position only if you have the right connections. In the U.S., by contrast, the culture is typically a meritocracy: your track record, not your connections, determines how far you can go. American managers put heavy emphasis on your performance. Donald Trump may not have gone to the top schools, he may not be well-liked, but his results as a real estate developer speak for themselves and qualified him, at least in the eyes of his supporters, to run for President—an unthinkable scenario in France.

- **Status** (hierarchical—democratic/participatory). Is there a steep hierarchy, or is the organization flat? How is social or economic status linked to gender, race, age, or religion? What are the status and power of women in the culture? For example, when Suzanne Daley arrived in South Africa as the new Johannesburg bureau chief for the New York Times and had directed the movers all day where to put the furniture, the foreman approached her and asked: "Where's the boss?" She responded with glee, "I'm the boss." He looked at her blankly; then he grew annoyed: "No. I mean the master." All the foreman wanted was a signature acknowledging that Daley and her husband had received their belongings, but her signature would not do. Finally, she shrugged. "He's in the back."[32]

French colleagues tell me that in their country, it is generally less important *what* you know than *whom* you know.

Is the style of leadership more "masculine" (hierarchical, structural) or more "feminine" (participatory, inclusive, organic)? In the U.S. managers often think nothing of bypassing their direct superior if producing the result warrants that. In fact you can score points by going directly to the top; it simply shows you are a resourceful leader. In France, the tradition of the absolutist state bureaucracy has created steep hierarchies, where bypassing your supervisor might be frowned upon and even seen as disloyal.

Other cultures have different motivations for conveying status. The Swiss assume that if you or your parents are not from the elite, you probably do not deserve to lead. In the British and Australian cultures, fairness is among the most esteemed values—and their idea of fairness is to bring down or speak out against those at the top in an attempt to even the playing field. (A British joke asks, what is the differ- ence between an American and a British worker? Answer: the American stands at the entrance of the GM fac- tory, sees the boss driving out in his Cadillac and says: "Goddammit, one day I'm gonna drive a Cadillac just like this!" Meanwhile, the British worker stands at the entrance of the Rolls Royce factory, sees the boss driving out in the Rolls and says: "Goddammit, one day this son of a bitch is gonna drive a bicycle just like me!")

In Eastern Europe, the former Communist regimes may have produced an absence of leadership and an aversion to risk.

- **Leadership** (team-oriented—independent, individualism— collectivism, initiative—waiting). How are decisions made? Is individual or group decision-making preferred? Who has decision-making power, and how do people know (by rank, title, seating arrangements, treatment by or of oth- ers)? Do people show personal initiative, even unilateral action, or do they wait or ask for permission? Should employees have opportunities to work together or to find solutions independently? Should individual performance be praised or criticized, or neither? Who is expected to take responsibility for breakdowns?

Leadership cultures differ from country to country, and often within countries. Americans have a profoundly dif- ferent mindset about leadership than people from Europe or Japan do. In the United States, leadership is seen as an adventure, and people want to be leaders. In contrast, in Japan, Sweden, and Germany, the emphasis is on group consensus. A brief look at the recent history of these countries tells why some cultures might consider it dangerous to stick your neck out too much. Japanese leadership led the country to destruction and humiliation in World War II. So today the Japanese put an emphasis on consensus that Americans consider absurd. For example, they hold staff meetings where everyone has to speak. I attended one that lasted two days, and the sleep I found myself fighting against was not just a result of jet lag. In Germany, defeat in both World War I and World War II has made people very reluctant to display leadership. Although Germany is a very powerful country, Germans shy away from overt leadership. Swedes have their own reason to shy away from leadership. Two outstanding and greatly admired leaders died violently in the second half of the twentieth century. Dag Hammarskjöld was killed in a plane crash, and Olaf Palme was assassinated. Given the already existing bias in the Swedish culture against exposing oneself as a leader—the Swedes even have a word for this, 'largom,' meaning something like 'the middle way'—it may well be that these violent deaths reinforced a cultural decision that leadership and sticking one's neck out are perilous. In Eastern Europe, the former Communist regimes may have produced an absence of leadership, an aversion to risk, and the expectation that the state, not its citizens, should provide leadership.

Western cultures tend to value self-interest much more than the East does. Descartes' famous dictum "I think, therefore I am" has led to a culture of me, mine, and money in the West. In Eastern cultures, such as in India, Japan, and China, the group is more important than it is in the West. For example, there is a strong norm that "we only do what the group says." Many people would gladly sacrifice themselves for their family or their company, even their country.

- **Change** (risk-averse—risk-friendly, continuity—discontinuity). Is change seen as an opportunity or a necessity? Are

people risk-friendly or risk-averse? Are
structures held as immutable or malleable? Are there sacred cows that cannot
be touched? How are new ideas best pre-
sented: by letter, e-mail, fax, phone, or in
a meeting? And by whom: by a senior
executive, by a project team, or by someone else? How loyal are people to each
other or to their company? What is
employee turnover? What is people's attitude toward leadership succession?

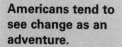

**Americans tend to
see change as an
adventure.**

People in the U.S. are much more mobile than in France, for
example. They move to Arizona or Florida, they change
employers, they even switch careers in the pursuit of
opportunity. Americans tend to see change as an adventure.

- **Space** (reserved—expansive; close—distant; boundaries—
  intimacy; order—chaos; open market—closed market).
  How important is privacy, or a personalized workspace?
  Are work and family distinct or overlapping? What are the
  attitudes toward order and disorder? Are first names, last
  names, or titles used? What is the role of nationality, status, gender, or race in building relationships? How open
  or closed is the economy? Is business an accepted topic at
  social occasions and vice versa?

Japan, for example, is a very small country with a lot of
people, so the Japanese are careful not to use space
unnecessarily. When they step into an elevator, many
Japanese will stand so close to the wall as to almost
become one with it. They will feel invaded by you if you
take up a lot of room. On the other hand, in the United
States, Canada, or Australia, people are accustomed to
having and using a lot of room, and the main street is
called "Broadway."

- **Communication** (indirect—direct; non-verbal—verbal;
  written—oral; self-expression —understanding; visceral—
  cerebral; silence—talking). Are differences discussed openly or behind closed doors? What is the best way to relate

information? How important is oral versus written communication? Should people voice their opinions or should they be silent? What do I say if I don't know the answer? What is the perception of silence? How do I apologize for a mistake?

For example, people in some cultures, such as in Britain or Switzerland, tend not to communicate directly, but to be roundabout. An American senior executive in the U.S. audit division of a major Swiss pharmaceutical company told me that she worked for two years in the UK office and enjoyed fairly cordial relations with her British colleagues. On the eve of her departure back to the United States, a key colleague told her brusquely that he had been completely dissatisfied with her work. She asked him, "Why didn't you tell me earlier?" He thought he had conveyed his displeasure, but she had never noticed. In general, British managers won't talk straight, at least compared to Americans and the Dutch, who love straight talk and get right to the point.

> In other cultures, especially in Europe, people's first priority is not to express themselves but to understand.

People in Sweden, Switzerland, and Japan are much more formal than they are in the U.S. As for companies, Dow Corning has a low level of formality, whereas the culture at Novartis, for example, is much more formal.

One facet of the communication dimension is self-expression vs. understanding. The culture in the United States, for example, is one of self-expression. Americans in general are used to expressing themselves, whether they love or hate something. They tend to speak their minds and express their opinions forthrightly and passionately. In other cultures, especially in Europe, people's first priority is not to express themselves but to understand. So if you do a sales presentation in Europe and people look very serious and are not responding at all, most likely they're extremely engaged and are trying to understand how what you're presenting works. In the U.S., silence might mean that your listeners are out to lunch.

- **Rules** (implicit—explicit; flexible—rigid; improvised—legalistic). Are rules or objectives clearly defined or left fuzzy? Are rules fixed, or can they be changed, and if so, how? Does an agenda need to be followed or can one deviate from it? Do people tend to comply with, or deviate from, agreements? What is the role of government, of unions?

> **The bottom line: If you do business with other cultures, adjust your pace.**

For example, in Sweden and the Netherlands people take promises very seriously. In these countries, if people promise something, they intend to deliver no matter what. They will do anything to avoid the disgrace of failing to deliver on their promises. This leads them to be cautious, understandably, in making promises. In other cultures, such as in Latin America and China, people might make promises or agreements more easily, and may be less obsessed with keeping them. In China, saying "yes" does not necessarily mean what it means in the U.S., since in China other values (loyalty, or contextual considerations, such as the background in which the "yes" was uttered) might weigh more than the promise itself.

In the U.S., there is a strong legal culture and a tendency to litigate. In other cultures, such as in Switzerland, people in general are more reluctant to use the courts to resolve disputes. If possible, the Swiss prefer to use informal gentlemen's agreements. The contracts they do use are minimal: a U.S. contract would be 25 pages long, but the equivalent Swiss contract might be only 10 pages.

Rules can extend into physical well-being or sexuality. What habits are permissible in a given culture? For example, how healthy is people's diet on average? How common is smoking? In Italy and Japan, the traditional diets are considered among the healthiest in the world, yet the people smoke like chimneys. In the United States, the typical diet is considered among the least healthy (nutrition writers use the acronym SAD for Standard American Diet to describe how Americans eat). Complimenting a female colleague on her attractive sweater might be perfectly acceptable in France, but lead to sexual harassment charges in the U.S.

- **Time** (long-term—short-term; past—future, rigid—loose; single-tasking—multi-tasking). Do people have a short or long-time horizon for decisions? Is age seen as positive (wisdom) or negative (outdated)? Are people punctual or not? How "dead" are deadlines? Is time seen as a malleable commodity or as uncontrollable? The concept of time is very different in India than in the United States. In India, people have an eternal and slow sense of time. When I lived in Bombay, I found the movies to be excruciatingly slow. If you were to make a promotional video for a South Asian audience, it would have to reflect this very slow pace. At the opposite extreme is the United States, where visuals and communications happen at a very high speed. The bottom line: if you do business with other cultures, adjust your pace.

Complimenting a female colleague on her attractive sweater might be perfectly acceptable in France, but lead to sexual harassment charges in the U.S.

Chapter Four

Making Global Meetings Work

The focus of this chapter is how to create, lead and debrief meetings effectively when the people on your team are spread out in different parts of the world. By "effectively" I mean that the meetings produce the results you want, that they enable co-creation, and that they result in alignment among the participants and the experience of partnership and team.

Before: Co-Creating the Agenda

Like any meeting, a virtual meeting is only as good as its preparation. You will have the videoconference for which you prepare yourself and the other participants. If you want to cause a breakthrough at a meeting, you better cause that breakthrough in the minds of a critical mass of participants beforehand.

- See the virtual meeting as a step in a process. Look at it not as an isolated event, but as an integral part of your company strategy for unleashing leadership.

Like any meeting, a virtual meeting is only as good as its preparation.

- Stand in the shoes of every participant. What are people's intentions, what are their concerns, what are their dreams? Stand in their shoes and see the world from their perspective. What might be important to Jim right now? What is important to the Mexicans?

- Co-create the purpose, intended results and agenda of the meeting. As much as possible, design the meeting with the people who will be participating. It works when you send a draft agenda to all participants before the meeting happens (make sure to call it a draft so they don't feel it is cast in stone). It works when they know the agenda beforehand. And it works when you ask participants what they think about the agenda.

- Pay attention to local time zones and local customs of the participants. Schedule the meeting so that it occurs during work hours for all the participants—or at least so that it's

Lead from the big picture, from your vision.

not in the middle of the night in Melbourne or on a national holiday in Venezuela. When you open the meeting, say, "Good morning, good afternoon, and good evening," or whatever the appropriate welcome would be given the locations of the participants. Also be aware of what season it is in the parts of the world where your participants are. A global teleconference can easily include New Yorkers who have battled a snowstorm to get to work and Argentineans who are leaving on their summer vacation the next weekend. Paying attention to such details will have the participants be more real for you.

During: Keeping Things on Track

- Lead from the big picture, from your vision. Don't let details get in the way of accomplishing your purpose and intended results. Human beings seem to be wired to be distracted by operational details. If an operational issue shows up during the meeting, get it handled off-line or create a task force to deal with it after the meeting.

- Speak and listen to every person as *the* key to the meeting. Whether it is the company's president or the company's receptionist, that person is the key to the success of the conference. So treat each and every person in the meeting that way.

- It helps to use a dose of British understatement and self-deprecating humor when you address a global audience. One example of this is Tim Melville-Ross, the director general of the Institute of Directors, who opened his speech to the institute's 1998 annual convention with these words:

> It is a real pleasure to speak to such a large and distinguished audience. If you will forgive me just a moment's conceit, it at least shows that in this respect my career has not been without progress. The first ever speech I made was in a village hall on a filthy February evening. It was cold, the wind was blowing, the snow was falling and there was just one other person present. I felt I owed it to the fellow to go ahead, so I made my speech and he applauded politely and I left the platform, put on my coat and was about to depart when I felt a hand on my shoulder. He said to me: "Please don't go—I'm the next speaker!" Thank you all for being here.

After: Leveraging the Momentum

- Complete the meeting by acknowledging everyone who made a key contribution to its success, including the agenda team, presenters, production team and people who produced materials.
- Debrief the meeting, both alone and with your agenda team. Ask these questions:
  - Did we accomplish the purpose of the meeting?
  - Which intended results did we achieve, and which not (and what is next in achieving the results we missed)?
  - What worked and should be done again in the future, and what did not work and should be avoided?
  - What promises and requests were made at the meeting, and who needs to be reminded?

- What, if anything, is incomplete for any of the participants?
- What about the meeting should be communicated to people who did not attend—how can they be empowered with the results or shared understanding of the meeting?
- And finally, what is next to keep up the momentum from the meeting?

What this chapter has covered is valid not only for global meetings or videoconferences, but for all vehicles for communication, from brochures to memos to a web site. Take web sites: since the Internet has no boundaries, how do you create a web site that can communicate as effectively to someone in New Delhi as it does to someone in New York? Very few web sites are truly global. The issue is not merely a matter of translating the words into different languages. Something that is hip in Silicon Valley may not communicate to people in London, much less to browsers in Rome and Moscow. Every time you miss the culture of an audience, you sacrifice an opportunity or might even do damage.

How do you create a web site that can communicate as effectively to someone in New Delhi as it does to someone in New York?

To construct a global web site, use focus groups that are truly global. Include someone from France, someone from Japan; make it representative of all the regions of the world where you expect to have a significant market. Then find out if the members of your focus group understand all the facets of your site and if they find any features confusing or off-putting. Find out if the site generates the response you intend to generate.

Traditional vs. Virtual Meetings

What is the difference between traditional sessions, where you meet your colleagues across the table, and a virtual meeting (a global conference call, an e-meeting or a videoconference)? And how do you choose the right medium?

First, in the traditional meeting you have more cultural cohesion. You sit face to face. There is a sense of intimacy. When participants sit across the room, there is immediate clarity. And when you say something, you can read their body language and see whether they understand what you are saying. When you speak to people over a TV screen, you cannot tell easily whether they follow what you are saying. This structural impediment leaves room for confusion and misunderstandings.

When I speak at a videoconference in New York and your line in Helsinki is muted, you probably perceive some inequality.

Second, in traditional meetings, there is perceived equality. What do I mean by that? When you and I sit across from each other, we have a sense of being one on one with each other, and we sit at the same table, so it does not feel as hierarchical, even when I speak and you don't. You could speak back any moment. But when I speak at a videoconference in New York and your line in Helsinki is muted, you probably perceive some inequality. I am in charge. I am running the meeting. I am sending the signals and you are forced to receive them (unless you hang up and bear the consequences). This leads to a certain recipient mentality on your part. You might feel that I'm doing it to you.

The third difference is social context. In a traditional session, there is a lot of social interaction and informality. We can crack jokes, I can ask something informally on the side, I can whisper to you, I can drop somebody a note on the side. By contrast, the virtual session tends to be more official, which leads to more diplomatic language and more formal interactions. And that makes it much more difficult to have the grease of relationship and social interaction.

Finally, in the traditional meeting, you are likely to interact with people with whom you have a background of shared relationship and shared practices. You feel at home. Your culture has become cohesive, and when you crack a joke, you can be reasonably sure

If you use sports analogies like "the whole nine yards," those statements may not be understood in German culture.

that your listeners will get it. In the virtual meeting, it is much more difficult. You are flying blind, and your ethnocentrism is revealed in a harsh light. You can no longer rely on the fact that what you say will be understood. You are unaware of the fact that your own cultural examples may not speak to the other culture at all. An example of that is if you use sports analogies like "the whole nine yards" or "move it down the field, Joe" or "let's kick their butt," those statements may not be understood in German culture. So when you use sports analogies, you may want to use analogies of universal sports like tennis, which people have understood in Germany ever since Boris Becker, or soccer rather than football if you speak to Brazilians or Russians. Alternatively, you might use a set of analogies that come from a global background so that any human being can understand, such as war analogies (but note that they may be inappropriate in Nordic countries!) or Chinese proverbs.

How you choose to communicate with colleagues spread out around the world is a strategic choice. Although virtual meetings are becoming the preferred way for keeping the global team in communication, they are not the only way. Traditional meetings still have their place. Let us look briefly at the advantages and disadvantages of virtual and traditional meetings.

The traditional meeting is the most expensive way for a global team to meet, so it will probably be used the least. It is travel intensive, and time intensive. Flying people from India to New York or London or vice versa is costly and takes valuable time. A two-day meeting in another country can easily consume a week when you include preparation, packing, travel, and jet lag. The opportunity costs can be enormous. Because of the high cost, the traditional meeting will usually occur less often and have fewer participants—usually just the key selected leaders of the organization.

Because it is less costly, a conference call or multi-point videoconference allows you to work with many more people at one time. I have been on teleconferences and videoconferences with more than 250 people, at a lower cost than holding a global meeting with 20 people in New York. You can also meet more frequently via videoconferencing than you can in person.

Rotate the meeting leadership so that people have a sense of shared ownership in these meetings.

Some have reservations about videoconferences as a communication medium. On a videoconference on this topic in 1999, one U.S. executive told me that in his company, it was virtually unimaginable that their Mexican colleagues would attend because "the Mexicans just don't like videoconferences." But that is nonsense. The question is, why were the Mexicans reluctant to use videoconferences? Is it that they never felt permission to shape the agenda and were constantly relegated to the receiving end? Is it that they felt imposed upon by the U.S. colleagues? I suggested to the executive to rotate the leadership of the videoconferences, and to invite his Mexican colleagues to lead some of them.

The traditional meeting lends itself to macro management, where you deal with strategic or major policy issues. The virtual meeting lends itself to hands-on management, where you roll up your sleeves and get to work on the tactics.

You may want to create an annual schedule of traditional and virtual meetings. Do this in a videoconference with all key members of your global team. Talk about how often you should have traditional meetings. Do you fly everybody to a global face-to-face only once a year or once every quarter? At the same time that you discuss when to have these meetings, also decide where to hold them. Try to meet in different locations around the world. That allows the members of your team to experience ownership of the whole organization when they host their colleagues, and to learn more from one another and about their opportunities and people as they visit each other's locations.

Also determine how often you want to schedule videoconferences, what the purpose of these virtual meetings will be, and who should attend them to fulfill that purpose. Rotate the leadership of the meeting so that people have a sense of shared ownership in them. If you have team members who do not want to participate in the videoconferences, invite them to be among the first to lead.

■ ■ ■

It would be a mistake to conclude from all the culture clashes above that companies should stay at home and not venture abroad. Even in the midst of recessions, many companies have pursued successful strategies for global expansion. But global managers must be culture-savvy. Let me leave you with a few recommendations as you embark on your own journey as a global citizen.

Recommendation #1: Immerse yourself in the target culture. On a promotional trip to China, Honeywell gave each inhabitant of a remote village a hooded yellow rain slicker with Honeywell's red logo. The only problem: it rarely rains in this hamlet of Handianzi. No one told Honeywell's CEO that the Chinese village's name means "very dry area."

Michael R. Bonsignore, chairman of Honeywell, has learned from that mistake. He logs 200,000 miles a year in travel outside the U.S. He has lived in five countries and speaks four languages. Even if you do not travel like Bonsignore, it pays to learn the language of another culture you do business with. As we saw above,

Heidegger said, "Language is the house of being." By learning the language, you learn the essence and thought patterns of a culture. And if you are not inclined to learn a language, then at the very least read a book, or watch a movie, that is cherished in that culture. Thomas Mann's Buddenbrooks will go a long way to explaining the German culture. Luchino Visconti's Il Gattopardo (The Leopard) will do the same for Italy.

Recommendation #2: Train your future leaders as global citizens. You will recall the cultural faux-pas committed by the U.S. military from the preface of this book, when American warplanes dropped thousands of food packages over Afghanistan in a goodwill gesture that backfired. The Pentagon responded quickly. Not only does the Pentagon's school, the Defense Language Institute, now offer intensive language courses, from Farsi to Pashto and Urdu, to some 3,500 students annually. A few months after 9/11, the top brass instructed the U.S. Military Academy at West Point to change its leadership development curriculum to include cross-cultural competency courses for its cadets.

Recommendation #3: Involve everybody in your global strategy—at the right time. Carlos Ghosn was born in Brazil, raised in Lebanon, and is a citizen of France. In 1999, he was sent to Japan by France's Renault S.A. when the company had bought 36.8 percent of Nissan. His mission: to restructure and revive the ailing Japanese car manufacturer. His promise: to post a profit for the fiscal year ending in March 2001. His process entailed closing factories, axing thousands of jobs and cutting off small, money-losing affiliates. This should have hardly endeared Ghosn to the Japanese, who are not exactly open to foreign managers. But the improbable happened: Ghosn succeeded, his autobiography sold 150,000 in the first month (just shy of the total attained by the first volume of Jack Welch's autobiography), and he has even become a comic book star—probably the highest honor in comic-crazed Japan.

What was Ghosn's main recipe for success? He recognizes the power of involving your global partners in creating your strategy. Many other managers do not—yet. Walmart, one of the most successful companies in the United States, failed to replicate its success in Germany, not only because its managers did not speak German, but also because it neglected to adopt basic German practices such as a strong partnership between management and trade unions. Walmart never created a strategy owned by the German managers, who are traditionally skeptical of foreign management. This would not have happened had the company invested in the global and intercultural competencies of its management. There is a growing understanding that few areas in today's business environment offer a greater return on investment. Today's leading managers know that for a minimal input, companies can make or save enormous amounts of money.

The Bottom Line

Companies lose enormous amounts of money because they fail to invest in their global competencies. (Coca-Cola lost billions in sales during the summer of 1999 because of its cross-cultural blindness.) These losses—through post-merger pains, missed opportunities, lawsuits, brain drain, etc.—are preventable through early and relatively low-cost investment.

- Globalization is a synergy of: (a) falling costs of communication and transportation; (b) the rise of the virtual team; (c) the breakdown of world Communism; (d) the rise of global media; (e) the Americanization of world culture; (f) the growth of multinational firms; and (g) the emergence of international organizations. Under globalization, all entrepreneurs and managers must be global citizens. They need to know what gifts to bring to dinner in Singapore and how to run a consensus-building meeting in Germany.

- Managers usually commit one or several of the 10 Capital Sins: (1) they think that the world plays by their rules; (2) they continue doing what they always did in the past; (3) they take English for granted; (4) they don't respect the cultural pathways for making things happen; (5) they don't stand in their host's shoes; (6) they forget to invest in relationships; (7) they jump from vision to action, forgetting about strategy; (8) they take the village by storm; (9) they forget that their advice is heard as mere noise unless they create a demand for that advice; (10) they choose the wrong people for overseas assignments.

- Managers can use four tools to prevent culture clash: Do's and Taboos of Global Citizenship, a set of general guidelines; Decoding Any Culture; the Global Results Pyramid™; and the Global Integrator™ Spider Graph.

- In mergers, acquisitions, alliances or joint ventures, the key things managers can do are to communicate their expectations clearly, to stand in the shoes of the other side and see the world from the other party's vantage point, and to look at cultural integration as an ongoing and separate business process, just like operations, marketing, or finance.

- Global meetings differ fundamentally from local, culturally cohesive meetings. For example, cracking the usual jokes or using U.S.-based sports analogies makes no sense.

Endnotes

1. *New York Times,* 13 August 2002. A16.
2. Reprinted verbatim from *The Economist, Sydney Morning Herald,* 1 October 2001.
3. Martin Buber. 1950. *The Way of Man: According to the Teachings of Hassidism.* London: Routledge and Kegan Paul.
4. Hyman Goldin. 1962. *Ethics of the Fathers.* New York: Hebrew Publishing Company. 10.
5. Rebecca West. 1941. *Black Lamb and Gray Falcon: A Journey Through Yugoslavia.* London: Penguin. 2.
6. Peter Drucker, "Management's New Paradigms," *Forbes,* 5 October 1998. 152–78.
7. Sources: United Nations, www.un.org; The Global Hunger Project Inc., www.thp.org; Population Reference Bureau, *World Population Data Sheet,* www.prb.org .
8. This concept has been going around the Internet. I am grateful to Brenda Dash for making me aware of it.
9. Adapted from The Hunger Project's *"Ending Hunger Briefing."*
10. *Christian Science Monitor,* 20 May 2000.
11. 10th annual *Human Development Report.* 1999. New York: UN Development Programme.
12. *New York Times,* 21 March 2001. A1.
13. Philip Martin; quoted by Stephen Castles and Mark J. Miller, *The Age of Migration: International Population Movements in the Modern World.* New York 1993: The Guilford Press. 2–3.
14. C.K. Prahalad and Kenneth Lieberthal, "The End of Corporate Imperialism," *Harvard Business Review,* July–August 1998. 69–79.
15. Benjamin Barber, *Jihad vs. McWorld: How Globalism and Tribalism are Reshaping the World.* New York 1995: Ballantine Books. 30.

[16] Prahalad and Lieberthal, *ibid.* 78.

[17] One book that highlights the battle between globalization and tribalism is Barber, *Jihad vs. McWorld.*

[18] Richard E. Nisbett, Kaiping Peng, Incheol Choi, and Ara Norenzayan, "Culture and Systems of Thought: Holistic vs. Analytic Cognition," *Psychological Review,* April 2001. Reviewed in *New York Times,* 8 August 2000.

[19] I owe these examples to Windham International, now GMAC, to *the Wall Street Journal,* and to Bill Bryson. 1996. *Made in America, An Informal History of the English Language in the United States.* New York: Avon Books.

[20] Stuart Crainer. "And the New Economy Winner is...Europe," *Strategy and Business,* Second Quarter 2001, 5.

[21] *New York Times,* 6 December 1998. A1.

[22] Interview in *Der Spiegel,* 3/1999. 90.

[23] *Fortune,* 22 November 1999. 237–248.

[24] *New York Times,* 8 July 2000. A1.

[25] *German American Trade,* 12:5. 39.

[26] *New York Times,* 17 May 2000. C1.

[27] Vijay Sathe. 1985. "How to Decipher and Change Organizational Culture," in: R. H. Kilman and Associates, *Managing Corporate Cultures.* San Francisco: Jossey-Bass.

[28] I am grateful to Nicholas Wolfson for bringing this article to my attention. First published in the *Arab Bulletin* #60, 20 August 1917; reprinted in *Lawrence's Secret Dispatches from Arabia* (1937), 126–133; reprinted in part in Basil Liddel Hart, *T.E. Lawrence.* 142–147. The original manuscript is in the PRO/FO 882/7.

[29] *Global Workforce,* November 1998. 9.

[30] Michael Bonsignore, *Financial Times,* 17 October 2001.

[31] This account is adapted from: Ronald N. Ashkenas, Lawrence J. DeMonaco, and Suzanne C. Francis. 1998. *"Making the Deal Real: How GE Capital Integrates Acquisitions." Harvard Business Review,* January–February. 165–178.

[32] *New York Times,* 11 October 1998.

Resources

Our clients often ask me if I can suggest tools or resources that could help them be more effective in dealing with people from other cultures. This section is my response to those requests. All the instruments and publications that I recommend here will help you better understand and deal with different cultures and their people.

The key is to immerse yourself, immerse yourself, and immerse yourself some more. If you are doing business with people from another culture, learn at least a little bit of their language. It goes a long way to establish trust if you can speak French or Spanish or Japanese. Read some books about that culture or by well-known authors from that culture. For instance, I suggest reading a novel by Thomas Mann if you want to do business in Germany or poems by Pablo Neruda to know more about Latin America. Read articles about the culture. If you don't like to read, watch movies about it, particularly movies filmed in that country in the native language. Do an Internet search about the culture. What you want to do is to see the world from that culture's point of view.

Several publications will give you a better idea of the cultures of different countries. One is the *World Press Review*. This excellent publication summarizes media coverage from around the world. Let's say you had a question about how President Clinton was perceived after Congress impeached him. How was he perceived in China? You could read what the *Beijing Express* wrote about this. How was he perceived in Australia? You could find out what the *Sydney Morning Herald* has to say. You get world coverage about any number of issues in every edition. This useful tool allows you to understand how people from other cultures think about particular economic, political, and social issues.

I also find the *Economist Intelligence Unit* valuable. This is a series of country briefings that, in a few pages, give you an overview of the culture, the geography, the history, the economics and the politics of a country. *EIU* also publishes a "Worldwide Cost of Living Survey" at www.eiu.com.

A resource that I recommend if you do a lot of business in Europe is *The Europeans,* a book by Italian journalist Luigi Barzini. It is a very entertaining book about culture. And even though it is about Europe, it gives you the tools for thinking about and decoding other cultures.

Another book series I recommend is *The Xenophobe's Guide to the....* Published by Ravette Publishing in the United Kingdom, it is a series of guidebooks, each on a particular culture, and each informative and entertaining.

Here is a list of books that I have found to be the most useful in my quest as a global citizen:

Axtell, Roger E. 1998. *The Do's and Taboos of Body Language Around the World.* New York: John Wiley & Sons.

Barber, Benjamin. 1996. *Jihad vs. McWorld.* New York: HarperCollins.

Barzini, Luigi. 1983. *The Europeans.* New York: Penguin.

Buber, Martin. 1974. *I and Thou.* New York: Scribner.

Friedman, Thomas. 2000. *The Lexus and the Olive Tree.* New York: HarperCollins.

Handy, Charles. 1995. "Trust and the Virtual Organization," *Harvard Business Review,* May–June. 40–50.

Heidegger, Martin. 1971. *On the Way to Language.* San Francisco: Harper & Row.

Hofstede, Geert. 2001. *Culture's Consequences: Comparing Values, Behaviors, Institutions and Organizations Across Nations* (2nd ed.). Thousand Oaks CA: Sage Publications.

Lipnack, Jessica and Jeffrey Stamps. 1997. *Virtual Teams: Reaching Across Space, Time and Organizations With Technology.* New York: John Wiley & Sons.

Morrison, Terri, Wayne A. Conaway and Joseph J. Douress. 2000. *Dun & Bradstreet's Guide to Doing Business Around the World.* Paramus, NJ: Prentice Hall Press.

Morrison, Terri, Wayne A. Conaway and George A. Borden. 1995. *Kiss, Bow or Shake Hands: How to Do Business in Sixty Countries.* Avon, MA: Adams Media Corp.

Nichols, Michael P. 1995. *The Lost Art of Listening.* New York: Guilford Publications.

Ohmae, Kenichi. 1990. *The Borderless World: Power and Strategy in the Interlinked Economy.* New York: HarperCollins.

Parker, Philip M. 1997. *Linguistic Cultures of the World.* Westport, CT: Greenwood Publishing Group.

Prahalad, C.K. and Kenneth Lieberthal. 1998. "The End of Corporate Imperialism," *Harvard Business Review,* July–August. 69–79.

Schein, Edgar. 1985. *Organizational Culture and Leadership.* San Francisco: Jossey-Bass.

Schell, Michael and Charlene Marmer Solomon. 1996. *Capitalizing on the Global Workforce: A Strategic Guide for Expatriate Management.* New York: McGraw–Hill.

Sen, Sondra. 2001. *Interacts. Business culture briefings for 40 countries.* Available at www.swissconsultinggroup.com.

Tomb, Howard. 1988. *Wicked French for the Traveler.* New York: Workman Publishing.

_____. 1992. *Wicked German for the Traveler.* New York: Workman Publishing.

_____. 1995. *Wicked Greek for the Traveler.* New York: Workman Publishing.

_____. 1988. *Wicked Italian for the Traveler.* New York: Workman Publishing.

_____. 1991. *Wicked Japanese for the Traveler.* New York: Workman Publishing.

_____. 1991. *Wicked Spanish for the Traveler.* New York: Workman Publishing.

Trompenaars, Alfons. 1997. *Riding the Waves of Cultures: Understanding Diversity in Global Business.* New York: McGraw–Hill.

Watzlawick, Paul. 2000. *Gebrauchsanweisung für Amerika.* München: Piper.

Zweifel, Thomas D. 2001. *Communicate or Die.* New York: Swiss Consulting Group.

_____. 2002. *Democratic Deficit? The European Union, Switzerland, and the United States in Comparative Perspective.* Lanham, MD: Lexington Books/Rowman and Littlefield.

Also, check out articles on cross-cultural HR management at www.workforceonline.com.

The Author

Thomas D. Zweifel (tdz@swissconsultinggroup.com) is a specialist in building and coaching global high-performance teams. The co-founder and CEO of Swiss Consulting Group (www.swissconsultinggroup.com) has lived on four continents and coached global leaders in Fortune 500 companies and small businesses, government and the military, non-governmental organizations and the UN since 1984. He and his clients achieved breakthrough results in the most diverse cultural environments—and often under adverse circumstances.

Born in Paris, Zweifel holds dual citizenship in Switzerland and the United States, and is fluent in English, German, French, and Italian. He holds a Ph.D. in International Relations from New York University, and teaches leadership in international and public affairs at Columbia University. Publishing frequently on leadership and democracy, global citizenship and communication, Zweifel is the author of *Democratic Deficit? The European Union, Switzerland, and the United States in Comparative Perspective* (Lexington Books, 2002) and *International Organizations: Democracy, Accountability and Power* (Lynne Rienner, 2003). He lives in New York City.

Your toughest time ever?

When I lived and worked in India, I almost died of a double infection—bacterial and amoebic at the same time. The doctor came and said: "You must go to the hospital." I said: "No, I have no time for this, I have work to do." He simply slapped me in the face and took me to Bombay Hospital. I was in a room with eight others, and all the religions of the world were represented in the room—Hindus and Buddhists and Catholics and Muslims, and there was wailing and praying night and day. A nurse sat next to my bed for nine days and nine nights. Along with losing almost all the water in my body, I hopefully lost some arrogance and gained some humility.

It took seven years to install a phone line while I lived in India. My task was to train fourteen local leaders to deliver a workshop across the nation. My efforts were frustrated at every turn. It was very, very hard, but I got the job done. As a consequence of our effort, millions of people have taken charge of their destiny and have uplifted themselves from the conditions of hunger.

Your worst job ever?
Once I was consulting an organization where no one listened to each other. It was almost physically painful to even be there. When people don't listen to each other, they jeopardize organizations.

Your greatest concern about the future?
Consumerism. My greatest fear is that we become passive, resigned, indifferent, self-centered individuals who have no interest in serving the community.

Your heroes?
Two leaders: Churchill, for embodying leadership and for reminding us that "We make a living by what we get, but we make a life by what we give." And Gandhi, whom Churchill called "that little naked man," for teaching us integrity. My favorite story about Gandhi is this:

Once, a mother traveled for many days—by train, by rickshaw, by bus and by foot—to bring her young son to Mahatma Gandhi. She begged, "Please, Mahatma. Tell my son to stop eating sugar."

Gandhi was silent for a moment. He said, "Bring your son back in two weeks." The woman was puzzled, but she thanked him and said that she would do as he had asked. She traveled all the way back to her village.

Two weeks later, she undertook the entire trip again—train, rickshaw, bus and foot—and returned with her son. When they stood before Gandhi again, he looked the youngster in the eye and said, "Stop eating sugar."

Grateful but bewildered, the woman asked, "Why did you tell me to bring him back in two weeks? You could have told him the same thing then."

Gandhi replied, "Two weeks ago, *I* was eating sugar."

Also by Thomas D. Zweifel...

- *Communicate or Die: Getting Results Through Speaking and Listening.* 2002. New York: Swiss Consulting Group.
- *Democratic Deficit? The European Union, Switzerland, and the United States in Comparative Perspective.* 2002. Lexington Books/Rowman & Littlefield.

Forthcoming...

- *Coaching Leaders: How to Unleash People Power and Performance.* 2003. New York: Swiss Consulting Group.
- *Strategy-in-Action: People-Centered Strategy that Gets Results.* 2003. With Tapas K. Sen Ph.D. New York: Swiss Consulting Group.
- *International Organizations: Democracy, Accountability, and Power.* 2003. Boulder, CO: Lynne Rienner Publishers.

Go to www.swissconsultinggroup.com to find out more and/or to join Swiss Consulting Group's mailing list. If you found any inaccuracies in this book, we would be grateful if you told us. Send an email to books@swissconsultinggroup.com or call us at 212-288-4858.